MW00325217

Titanic Thompson

Stroke of Genius

Richard Campbell

Titanic Thompson
Stroke of Genius

For

Lorena and Harry
Linda
Stewart and Wylie

Chapter 1

In The Beginning
There Was...
Bad Luck.

In a rural Arkansas cabin, near the White River in 1897, five-year-old Alvin Clarence Thomas slept peacefully with his small puppy, Ace, cradled in one arm.

They were both suddenly awakened by the sound of loud voices in the next room. Quickly, a frightened Alvin picked up his puppy, climbed out of bed and tiptoed to the bedroom door. In the cabin's sparse front room, Alvin saw his mother, Sarah, pleading with his father, Lee. The argument was indistinct, but the tone was obviously painful, especially for the young boy listening.

Suddenly, as if he had just reached a decision, Lee grabbed a saddlebag and bolted for the door. A frightened Sarah was right behind him.

Alvin rubbed his eyes and surveyed the now empty front room. A spent whiskey bottle rested on the small dinner table and a still-burning cigarette lay on the edge of it.

He heard sounds of sharp voices coming from outside, so Alvin headed toward the front door with his puppy still in his arms.

Outside in front of the house, Sarah Thomas stared stoically at her husband as he mounted his horse then took a gulp from a full bottle of whiskey. Though swaying unsteadily in his saddle, Lee was still able to make out Alvin approaching his mother's side.

"Smart. Oh, he's a smart one all right. Ain't that what you always say, woman?"

Lee took another drink, as Sarah cast an eye on Alvin. Then, she braced herself for the worst which she sensed was coming and tried again. "Lee. Lee! Look at me! I'm beggin'. Just come back inside and think on it–tomorrow things will look..."

"Tomorrow?" he said as he took another drink for courage, again swaying precariously in the saddle. "Sarah! You ain't workin' your way with me no more!"

He nearly fell out of the saddle, but managed to catch himself, albeit clumsily. "No Ma'am," he continued. "No way! No shape! No form! No fashion!"

Fighting both her tears and her fears, Sarah pulled a frightened Alvin close to her side. Mother and child could only look on and watch Lee's tirade which gushed out of him as if to wash away his guilt. "No Ma'am! No more bein' tied to a youngen and a wife–a wife who nags and only wants a husband who can bring home regular pay."

"Lee, I said it was the gamblin' that hurt us. That and the–" she caught herself and stopped just short of mentioning the whiskey. "You always tried to do right, but–"

"Well, maybe I can't make a livin' here, but I can in the city." He sounded as though he was trying to convince himself as much as Sarah when he said, "I'm a gambler. And a damned good one. The kind that can sure make a fortune in New York City."

As only a drunk can do, he then seemed to change personalities in a split-second. In a pleading voice he said to Alvin, "Son, I plan on trying to help you and your Ma from time to time, just as soon as I start winnin'."

Sarah raised her fist to her mouth in anguish. For the first time, she realized her Lee was really going.

Lee's eyes never left Alvin as his personality and tone changed, yet again. This time he was cold. "But don't count on it, Alvin Clarence Thomas. Don't ever count on nothin' from me or anybody else. 'Cause in this life, if somethin' can go wrong– it will!"

As if performing a final ritual of passage, Lee raised one finger to his forehead in a half-hearted salute to his son, turned his horse toward his uncertain future, and rode off into the darkness.

Sarah watched, frozen in disbelief. With glistening eyes, she held her Alvin even closer. But, suddenly, as if a thunderbolt had struck her, she turned and ran frantically into the farmhouse.

She reached the kitchen where she threw herself down on her knees and thrust her hand frantically inside the deep recesses of the lower shelf–her fingers aching to touch an ordinary tin can, but a very special one–where she had hidden every penny she had.

Finding the tin can, she pulled it out and slowly, almost knowingly, she turned it upside down. There was nothing there.

Sarah was not a cruel or vengeful woman. Yet, the words she uttered at that moment could only be described as those of cold hatred.

"Lee Thomas. Have you no shame?"

Chapter 2

He Didn't
Have Rocks
in His Head.

On a particularly beautiful fall morning six years later, a flock of geese raced wildly across the surface of the crystal clear White River, each splashing awkwardly as it struggled to gain altitude.

Finally, just at the instant it appeared it would not, each succeeded in defying gravity, triumphantly rose into the air, and in the process, was instantly transformed into grace personified.

When they all had gained precisely the same altitude, they quickly and instinctively left all pretense of individuality behind and obediently combined to create a disciplined formation, etching an almost perfect V on the autumn canvas of that endless Arkansas sky.

Then as one, they rose majestically–higher and higher–and flew into the distance until they were almost out of sight. But suddenly they turned, circled back to where they had risen, and dipped their wings as if to say goodbye. Goodbye to the river below. And goodbye to the beautiful, yet pitifully poor Ozark countryside.

The formation turned Southeast, picked up speed, quickly reached a nearby mountain crest, passed over it–and was devoured by a huge ball of white flame burning on the horizon.

Though they were gone from sight, for a long while their cries continued to bank off the surrounding mountain walls and drift faintly back. And they were melancholy cries, which strangely, disguised the joy of their departure.

Far below, the crystal clear water of the river churned a restless rhythm. As if afraid it was being left behind, it quickly made its obligatory, fleeting appearance–then also roared eagerly away.

One glance beyond the river's bank, and it was obvious why everyone and everything wanted out of this place. A small apple orchard. A weathered barn. A tired old mule. They all stood as silent reminders that times were hard in this place.

Looking several hundred yards away–up past the sloping bank–there was a clearing, where a shabby old farmhouse stood. It was still sturdy but badly in need of paint.

The same might have been said for Sarah Thomas, the woman who stepped out on the front porch that morning. Not yet thirty, she already looked time-worn. But, even in her drab, homemade clothes and prematurely gray-streaked hair, she was still stubbornly attractive. Even a quick look at her showed that there was no quit in her. And certainly no foolishness.

With her hands shading her eyes, Sarah quickly searched the area for something. Then she raised both hands to her mouth and yelled in a practiced way, "Alvin. Alvin Clarence Thomas!"

In exasperation, she muttered to herself, "Now–where is that boy?"

Down by the river–conveniently out of sight, but not out of his mother's mind–was Alvin Clarence Thomas, now a ramrod-straight, eleven-year-old, with piercing dark eyes. He and his now grown dog, Ace, both stood looking, questioningly, at a man named Buck Bostwick.

Fat, fortyish, and dressed well-to-do, Buck looked out of place on the riverbank where in his hand he held a rock about the size of a hen's egg. He studied it carefully, almost painfully.

As though he had just made up his mind about something, Buck took a final look at his own rod and reel leaning against a nearby tree along side young Alvin's rifle. He looked around to make sure no one could hear. Then, in a voice which sounded as if he had just stumbled upon the wisdom of the ages, he declared, "Damn! You are one smart boy because you got it! And you got it the very first time I explained it to you! See! That is exactly what making a bet is all about!"

Again Buck looked around to make sure no one was watching, then he continued.

"Two people disagree over something–like you and me do now–so they both put up something of value. Me? Well, I put up my expensive, special-delivery, Montgomery Ward mail order rod and reel over there."

He pointed at his rod and reel leaning against the tree.

"And you? Well, you only have to put up that little old, good-for-nothing rifle a yours."

He pointed at Alvin's pitiful gun.

Wide-eyed and genuinely excited at the proposition before him, Alvin quickly interjected, "Then, we hold a little contest–kinda like a game–and the winner gets everything? That right? The winner gets both things?"

Buck appeared to be ecstatic at the sheer genius of the youngster.

"Exactly! That is exactly correct! That way, we can find out if that dog of yours really can fetch up this rock from the bottom of that river."

Alvin was suddenly serious as the mettle of his dog was challenged. "Oh, he can all right."

With a different, sharply impatient tone, Buck answered, "Aww hell, fetchin' a stick is one thing, boy. But no damn dog, no damn where, can do what you're..."

He quickly caught himself, and with a

reassuring smile, he extended his hand with the sincerity of someone extracting a blood oath.

"Then we–we do have a bet? Is that right?"

Filled to the brim with that naive confidence which only the young possess, it was all Alvin could do to contain himself as he winked knowingly at an anxious Ace, then quickly extended his hand to Buck.

"Heck, yes! I mean–Yes, sir!"

With the formalities of the hand shake completed, Buck quickly dropped Alvin's hand and also his well-practiced "good old boy" act. It was time to carve this deal right down to the bone.

A wicked smile crept over Buck's face as he said coldly, "Now, let's just wait a damn minute. Here's the thing. If your mutt was to bring up a rock from the bottom of that river, how would an honest man like me ever know, for sure, that he'd brought up the exact same rock that you threw out there in that big old river?"

Alvin's face looked like his very life's blood had been drained. After a long, painful moment– defeated and mortified–he could only say, "Well, I...uh...I guess...I guess..." as he looked sadly at Ace, hoping for a miracle. But, the remorseful dog was, of course, no help in a situation like this. But he could do what he had been taught–tricks. So, gamely, Ace slid down to a praying position on the ground.

With certain resignation that the game was

already over, Alvin said quietly and evenly, "I reckon, Mister, I reckon that you want me to mark that rock? Is that what you're gettin' at?"

Buck was already nodding as he said in a voice dripping with sarcasm, "Damn! Now there's a good idea!" He tossed the rock to Alvin who reluctantly but carefully marked a large "X" on it, and then showed it to a smiling Buck.

Alvin knelt down, put his hand under Ace's chin, looked him dramatically in the eye, and said sadly, "It's over, Ace. This man's got us for sure. Anyways, you get on out there and do your level best."

With that, Alvin hurled the rock far out into the river, and in a pleading voice, said loudly, "Ace! Fetch!"

On Alvin's command, Ace leapt obediently, almost suicidally into the river. The dog swam directly out to the exact spot where the rock had entered the water, and then dived beneath the surface.

A smiling, confident Buck took the moment to cast a covetous eye on Alvin's rifle. *It ain't much, but I can get some use out of it*, he thought, with a smile. But the smile quickly faded when he saw Ace reappear with a rock clinched tightly between his teeth, paddle quickly back to shore and drop the rock at Alvin's feet.

From where he stood, Buck could clearly see that the rock definitely had an "X" marked on it.

And, even though that small rock Ace dropped at Alvin's feet landed with a gentle "plop" on the soft, moist ground next to the water's edge–to Buck, it landed with a noise as deafening as an anvil being pounded in his ears.

Not only that, but the absolute and utter shock of the moment's events, created an adrenaline rush which careened wildly throughout Buck's body, pressuring his heart to a triple-time beat.

Even in this dysfunctional state, Buck was able to recognize that it was a totally different Alvin Thomas who picked up the rock. Oh, he was, of course, still barely eleven years old, but that was only in earth time. To Buck, he now seemed older. Much older. The wide-eyed enthusiastic child had given way to a quietly, coolly efficient young businessman, who calmly showed the rock to an astonished Buck, in much the same way a doctor might show a terminal patient an X-ray of his inoperable tumor.

One second, painful glance at the rock, and Buck again saw the large "X" clearly marked on it like a scarlet letter.

Strangely, Buck simply smiled and nodded affirmatively, even admiringly, as he said, "Well I'll be damned! I'll just eternally and most surely be damned!"

With that, he tossed the rock on the ground, carefully picked up his rod and reel, and turned to leave. Over his shoulder he sheepishly said, "One thing's for sure, Alvin Thomas. If we ever decide to do that bet for real, I'll damned sure be more respectful of that dog of yours!"

The time for fun and games was long over, so a serious Alvin picked up his rifle, cocked it, and pointed it directly at the retreating Buck.

Hearing the cock of the rifle, a hesitant Buck stopped, turned, and saw the weapon aimed directly at him.

"Hey! Come on now! You know we was both just funnin'," Buck said, almost pleading.

But Alvin would have none of it. "A bet's a bet, Mister. Now that's my expensive, special delivery, Montgomery Ward mail order rod and reel you're holdin'. Now, give it to me!"

Shaken at young Alvin's bravado–and memory–Buck's face turned beet red as he threw the rod and reel at Alvin's feet. Forgetting for a moment who had the gun, Buck hissed, "Why you backwoods white trash. You ain't nothin'. Do you hear me? You're 'bout as worthless as that good for nothing daddy of yours that up and ran off without payin' his gamblin' debts."

Cursing Alvin and his father under his breath, Buck turned and stalked off.

Buck had wounded the boy. Red-faced, Alvin extended an invitation. "Hey! Come on back and put some real cash money down! I'll bet you Ace can do it again!"

The defeated Buck didn't have the courage

or even the slightest inclination to turn and face Alvin and his rifle again. Instead he continued his retreat and shouted loudly and bitterly over his shoulder, "Sure, I'll bet you again, kid. When hell freezes over! Do you hear me? When hell freezes over!"

For a second, Alvin looked after the retreating Buck. Then, he relaxed, marveled at his new rod and reel, and looked down at his faithful Ace, who had come over as if to congratulate him. He rubbed the dog's head and said with sincere gratitude, "Atta boy."

At that moment, Sarah Thomas arrived on the scene. She looked at the quickly departing Buck Bostwick in the distance, then at Alvin, then at the new rod and reel–and she looked at it in a way that only a mother can.

Her look was not lost on Alvin, and especially not on Ace, who became agitated and seemed to cower, then he executed small, excited circles before finally sliding to the ground in a pose of total subservience.

But it was Alvin who gained Sarah's total attention. She picked up the expensive-looking rod and reel and turned to him. "Alvin! Tell me. How did you get this fancy thing?"

"Won it in a game with Buck Bostwick," he said in an even voice. He played no games with his mother.

"Game?"

"Yessem."

She looked at him thoughtfully, and then she spoke, very slowly. "Alvin, listen and listen careful! Games are for Buck and his kind. People like us–we have to put business 'fore pleasure."

Alvin looked confused, as if he had been missing something for a long time, and he had. "Business? What's our business, Ma?" he asked.

Sarah looked Alvin straight in the eye and made her point quietly but emphatically.

"Survivin'."

She started back up the hill toward the house. For a long moment, Alvin looked after her. Then, with a relieved smile, he picked up the marked rock and hurled it toward the same spot in the river where Ace had fetched it earlier. But, Alvin did not issue the "fetch" command Ace was always ready for.

Ready to go–but more anxious to please Alvin–Ace restrained himself as the rock plopped once again into the water and quickly sank to the sandy bottom. The rock came to rest very near where it had come to rest earlier–among at least fifty other rocks, all approximately the same size.

Interestingly, each and every rock had also been very carefully marked with the exact, same sized "X."

Chapter 3

Medals Day.
A Day Which
Would Live In
Infamy.

If young Alvin Thomas had a favorite school day, it was Medals Day, a day of scheduled athletic events including running, jumping and throwing– with the winner of each event receiving a shiny silver medal. But, if one contestant won more events than anyone else, he received the coveted gold medal. Of course, everyone knew the medals weren't real silver or gold, but they were very precious to all those youngsters who tried to win them. And try they did.

But, as Alvin had gotten older, his fast-developing athletic skills made him the odds-on favorite to win every event. In fact, as one boy said, "Heck. If Alvin's not sick, what's the use of showin' up?"

Still, on Medals Day in 1905–Alvin Thomas or not–men, women and children showed up from all over the county to witness the event. It was held at the small, white, one-room schoolhouse nestled in a clearing of a dense, wooded area several miles from Alvin's house.

To reach the school, most people used a wooden bridge that crossed the high-banked creek which meandered past the school. But that year, a spring storm had washed the bridge away, so anyone coming from the wrong direction had to travel several extra miles to another bridge down stream, or use a rope swing attached to a huge elm tree on the far bank to cross the water. But some did it, and did it gladly, because this was the biggest day of the school year.

The events were held on the leveled playground next to the school, and the site was marked by a huge banner which hung overhead and proudly proclaimed: MEDALS DAY.

The earlier competitions of the day had ended much the same as they had the year before–with Alvin winning. And, as an excited group of men, women, girls and boys screamed, Alvin Thomas easily won the premiere and final event of the day, the foot race.

Near the finish line, Buck Bostwick stood with his unhappy wife, Adele. They frowned as their portly son, Donald Dean–the biggest kid in school–finished a distant second, staggering across the finish line far behind Alvin.

Buck and Adele anxiously hurried over to the finish line where Alvin, bright-eyed and flushed with victory, proudly stood next to the school's only teacher, Miss Irene Sullivan, who was supervising the events. Miss Sullivan had genuine admiration as she handed the silver medal to Alvin and said, "Well done, Alvin. Very well done."

"Done is right," Buck whispered under his breath to Adele. Miss Sullivan turned to the crowd, held the gold medal high for everyone to see, and proclaimed loudly, "The winner of the gold medal is Alvin Clarence Thomas!"

Just as she hung the gold medal around Alvin's neck, Buck stepped up and said, "Well, young Thomas. Ain't seen much of you lately."

Alvin eyed Buck with earned suspicion, as he answered, "Spend most of my time workin' my mule."

Buck smiled and said insincerely, "Shame you can't win again this year, boy." Then quickly, and with great satisfaction, Buck removed the gold medal from around Alvin's neck.

Miss Sullivan was stunned. She stepped directly up to Buck and said, "Can't win? Why, of course he can. Alvin clearly won."

But, Buck had other plans. "Now Miss Sullivan. He can't win this year if last year he won ever contest! The run–the throw–the jump–everything! That's the rule!"

Buck pointed at Alvin as if he were guilty of something, and said, "The new rule."

Miss Sullivan's face turned scarlet. "New rule? The new rule! There is no new rule, and if there were, it would have to be approved by the school board."

Buck smiled. He was enjoying this. "Now Miss Sullivan. The kinda money I put into this school–including the price of these medals–says I am the school board. And now, accordin' to the new rule, which states–you just can't win if you won the same thing last year–the medal goes to the second place runner, which just happens to be my son, Donald Dean!"

To Miss Sullivan's utter dismay, a smiling Buck hung the medal around Donald Dean's neck. Adele Bostwick took a wicked look at Alvin, then beamed as she gazed at the light of her life, the pudgy, out-of-breath, Donald Dean.

Strangely, no one in the entire crowd–other than Miss Sullivan–raised any objection to Buck's rule or even offered one word in Alvin's defense.

In fact, the other contestants gathered around Donald Dean in a show of support. As a group, they looked vengefully, even hatefully at Alvin who answered them with a cold, hard stare. It was the first time in his life that Alvin had seen the monster of jealousy and envy released. But, it would not be the last.

Miss Sullivan read the situation clearly and

knew a terrible wrong had been planned and carried out. But she also knew it was all far beyond her ability to rectify. Instead, she turned her attention to Alvin and tried to comfort him by privately saying, "I am so very, very, sorry."

Alvin just nodded, turned away and motioned for his dog, who was sitting obediently under a tree.

"Come on, Ace," he said dejectedly, as he strode purposefully away from the school with the sound of the others cheering for the new champion still ringing in his ears.

With Ace at his side, Alvin walked slowly, thoughtfully home–past plowed fields, across a dry-weather crossing, and through a stand of oak trees that stretched as far as his eyes could see.

Arkansas was as verdant and beautiful as Alvin's mood was black.

———————————

Later that night, Sarah Thomas sat with her son at the crude wooden table in the front room, lit by a kerosene lantern. Ace lay on the floor next to Alvin's foot, chewing on a bone Alvin had just dropped on the floor for him.

Sarah was deeply concerned for her son and what had happened that day. But she knew it was a chance to teach her son a lesson he might need later, so she leaned in and spoke evenly. "Buck

Bostwick thinks his havin' money gives him a license to carry brains. Ain't so. Anyways, a medal doesn't make Donald Dean Bostwick the winner. The one who crosses the finish line first–medal or not–he's the winner."

"Not today, Ma."

"Alvin. Buck had to change the rules for his son to win. That boy will be countin' on his daddy to change the rules for him for the rest of his life."

"Well, I could beat 'em all, if I could just make them play by the rules."

"It ain't likely, Alvin. Ain't likely at all."

"Then maybe I'll have to make up my own rules."

Sarah could only guess at what was going around in her son's fertile mind at that instant. So, she said nothing, but just looked at him tenderly. She knew she did him no favor by coddling him– she had never done that–so she judged him in her mind, maybe a bit harshly, but also fairly. But that was for his own good. *No*, she thought, *he'll get no favors now, 'cause he'll get none out in the world.*

It was a hard world, she knew, and few things in it had more value than the truth. So, it was the truth he would get from her. The most valuable gift she could give him.

It was already obvious to her that he had the mind, the body, and most of all, the spirit to get ahead–to succeed somewhere, at something. And she knew he would need all of those things–and a lot more–just to get out of the Ozark mountains, where so many people had been born, lived their entire lives, and died without ever having a chance to see any of the other world–the one outside.

Yes, she knew it would take more, including some important things his father, Lee, never had–like mental strength and focus. Although she knew the odds were against her boy, and it would not be easy, she also knew from what he had already accomplished, her Alvin had a chance to go a long way in this world. A lot further than most.

And she sensed, as only a mother can, that he was already well on his way.

Chapter 4

Good-bye
To The Ozarks.

Although life was simple, slow, and seemed always the same in the Ozarks, newspapers from St. Jo brought news of a world war, far off in Europe. As she watched older boys head off, Sarah knew the day was coming when she would be forced to say goodbye for the very first time to her son.

In the spring of 1918, that day came. So Sarah and Preacher Otho Harkrider–a thin, white-haired, gentle man–accompanied Alvin to the river and stood with him next to a barge that would be taking Alvin and others away.

Among the small crowd of people who had come to see their loved ones off, Sarah stood and gazed fondly at her son, now a young man–straight, tall, darkly handsome and still intensely serious.

With no father to give advice, it had fallen to Preacher Harkrider to instill the wisdom which could only be given man-to-man. Harkrider knew Alvin wasn't just going to war, he was also going to meet that outside world, and there were things he needed to know. So, they had talked of wine, women and song–and also diseases, what things cost, and even a little etiquette, like pulling a chair out and where a napkin goes. Not much, but all useful things for a young man out on his own for the first time. And Preacher Harkrider wanted to make sure his lessons had been not only learned but understood.

"Now Alvin, remember what we've been talkin' about these past few days. The ways of the outside world are something mighty strange to us folk."

"I'll do exactly like you told me and get a lay of the land before I stretch my neck out," Alvin assured him. The preacher looked satisfied.

Alvin looked at Sarah. "You know I'll be careful."

She could only nod as she fought her tears.

Even though the rope lines had been cast off, and the barge was starting to slowly move away, Preacher Harkrider was not through. "Remember, Alvin. God helps them that help themselves."

"Don't worry. I plan on helping myself," Alvin agreed.

With a questioning look, Sarah managed a smile.

As the barge's whistle blew, Alvin quickly

tossed his one bag on the boat and then turned and shook the preacher's hand.

Then, he faced Sarah. She held his face in her hands, but she was still unable to speak. She simply kissed him tenderly.

"I gotta go, Ma. Don't worry. Don't worry about a thing."

Her tears were flowing, as he turned away from her, and stepped out on the barge, now moving away a bit faster.

Everyone in the small crowd at riverside was trying to shout last minute goodbyes to their loved ones, so when Sarah finally found her voice, she had to yell over everyone for Alvin to hear her last instructions.

She walked along the bank, speaking loudly, "Alvin! Whatever you do, don't be weak like your daddy! No drinkin'! Swear it!"

As if repeating a vow, Alvin yelled, "No drinkin'! I swear."

She wasn't through. "No smokin'!"

"No smokin', ma!"

"And above all–no gamblin'!"

Alvin blinked. He just stared at his mother in silence as he drifted farther and farther away.

Almost beside herself, she screamed, "Alvin Clarence Thomas! Did you hear me? I said no games of chance!"

Alvin relaxed, and smiled broadly. "Sure, Ma. I promise. No games of chance!" Then quietly to himself he said, "Ain't nobody gonna have a chance but me."

He waved again and watched Sarah Thomas and Preacher Harkrider growing smaller and smaller on the shore. The barge moved around the bend, and suddenly they were out of sight.

But one thing was for sure. Sarah Thomas would never be completely out of her son's mind which raced a mile a minute as he looked down river where he knew–for better or for worse–the outside world and his future in the United States Army awaited him.

Chapter 5

The 100% Absolutely Guaranteed Sure Thing.

Though it was an early winter in November of that year–the one thousand, nine hundred and eighteenth year of our Lord–it didn't feel all that cold in Anniston, Alabama. Not cold at all.

And that's exactly what the United States Army had counted on. After all, they had to train the soldiers who would be asked to take the place of those other young Americans who were dropping like flies on those European battle fields, whose names you could barely pronounce. So, what better year-round training place could you name?

Not Michigan. No, it was a given that every winter, someone's butt would have to be pried loose from an outhouse seat where it had been frozen.

And not Illinois. Especially not near Chicago with its lake effect sleet, snow and horrendous cold. No, not Chicago, where a gangster's body could be disposed of in a hole in the ice of almost any nearby lake, and never float up, or even be discovered from beneath the ice, until sometime after the first thaw, which sometimes didn't happen way up north until late May.

No. If you were going to correctly train your young men to use their rifles in order to blow the living hell out of the Kaiser's troops, it would require rifle practice hour after hour, day after day, on a rifle range which–even in the dead of winter– wasn't covered in ten feet of snow.

So it was there in Anniston, far below the Mason-Dixon line, that these new, young, raw recruits found themselves on that November day in 1918. And as they stood in a line, firing their rifles at circular targets far in the distance, two older men–career sergeants, Wilkie and Durham– stood nearby, smiling like two cats about to lick the cream.

The staccato sounds of random rifle shots provided a convenient background which drowned out their conspiratorial conversation. Wilkie, a short man with beady eyes, was barely able to control his self-satisfaction as he rubbed his hands and said smugly, "Well, this oughta teach young private Thomas the danger of letting his mouth overload his ass."

His confidant, Sergeant Durham, older and downright mean-looking, could only smile and agree. "That's sure as hell the God's truth. 'Course, if you go around braggin' about bein' the best shot in camp, you better damn well know that one day, somebody just might challenge you to back it up."

"And that somebody just might be the company's regimental rifle champion." Stifling a laugh, Wilkie inhaled too quickly and almost gagged on his chaw of tobacco.

"Who we are backin' one hundred and ten percent!" said Durham.

Barely able to control their laughter, they both ducked their heads and gasped for breath.

Durham recovered first. "Well, at least we showed him good old Christian charity by givin' him three to one odds."

"But hell, even at that, this'll be the easiest damn money we ever made."

This thought rekindled their pent up laughter. Realizing that both were nearly out of control, Durham managed to gather himself, then after carefully looking around to make sure that no one had heard, he raised one finger to his lips.

"Loose lips sink ships."

Wilkie nodded seriously. He knew their financial prospects were so large, and so sure, the only thing that could go wrong was if they were careless and gave their brilliantly conceived plan away.

He regained his composure and with a dead serious expression looked at two distant figures walking toward them. He pointed in their direction, "Speakin' of ships, looks like ours is coming in!"

Durham looked in the direction Wilkie pointed. Far away, at the end of the rifle range, Private Alvin Thomas and the camp's Regimental Rifle Champion were purposefully striding toward the group of men. Eyes straight ahead. Rifles in hand.

The Champ, about thirty-five years old, was an obvious spit-and-polish, no-nonsense type.

In contrast, Alvin, slender and tall–much taller than the Champ–looked to be in his mid-twenties and walked with that special ease and casualness borne only of a natural athlete. But it was only with a close look that you could see the real difference between the two men.

There was something about Alvin's eyes. They were dark. Maybe a bit small, but intense. Like that of a deer caught in a headlight.

And cold. So very cold like that of a northern winter. And it was only through those eyes that one could sense the carefully guarded intensity within him. And, the danger.

But it was a different Alvin Thomas that carefully chose the exact words to address the Champ at that moment. A well rehearsed one.

"This is a real honor. I mean, here I am,

shootin' against the champion of the regiment."

He whistled softly to himself, as if this had been his life's goal. "The whole damn regiment!"

He looked at the Champ with unabashed awe and respect.

"You really must be something!"

The Champ had no reason not too, so he easily and quickly bought the flattery. In fact, he enjoyed and maybe even expected it.

With false modesty he replied, "Well, I guess you could say I've done okay."

Not caring, but feeling he should say something, he offered, "What did you say your name was, kid?"

Alvin seemed almost overcome with gratitude that the Champ would even speak to him, as he blurted out, "I'm Alvin Thomas! Plain old Alvin Clarence Thomas out of Arkansas, Rogers, Arkansas."

"So, uh, Thomas, do much shootin' back home?"

"Oh, well, nothin' much. At least, nothin' compared to what you've done."

Alvin waited a calculated moment, then stole a glance at the Champ as he said, "You know, I was just thinkin'. With all the competitions you've won, I'll bet you ain't got a nerve in your whole body." He held a finger in the air. "Not even one."

"Yeah. I'm used to competition all right. You gotta be if you wanna win medals like these," he said, as he pointed proudly at the cluster of medals on his shirt.

Alvin whistled as he looked a little too admiringly at the Champ's medals. "Oh yeah. Damn! I see whatcha mean."

Another calculated pause.

"And I'll just bet you sure as hell have put away a lot of money."

Alvin looked around to make sure no one was listening, as he lowered his voice. "Come on, you can tell me. How much money have you won shootin?"

"Well, I haven't won any money," a little irritated that Alvin would ask. "Like I say, I shoot for medals!"

Alvin persisted, "You always shoot for medals, huh? So, you don't ever shoot for money?"

Now the Champ was getting pissed. His eyes quickly darted to Alvin as he said, "Look kid. I shoot. I win. I get the medals! What the hell difference does it make what I shoot for?"

Alvin's face reflected something that was obviously disturbing him greatly. "Oh, nothing. Nothing 'cept..."

" 'Cept what?"

" 'Cept, well, if you'd lost, you wouldn't a lost anything, would you?"

"Well, I'd have lost the medal if, and I repeat, if I'd have lost!"

Alvin shook his head in wonderment. "You

see, that's just the thing. You can't lose somethin' you never had. I mean the medal never was yours to start with. So if you'd have lost, you wouldn't have lost the medal. You just never would a got it. See what I mean?"

Though he tried to act casual, that thought seemed to strike a resonant chord somewhere very deep within the Champ, who muttered almost to himself, "Well, yeah. I guess you could look at it that way."

At that moment, there was suddenly a noticeable difference between the two contestants. The Champ, captured by the constant chatter of the younger man, seemed to hang on Alvin's every word, as if some age old truth was being explained to him for the very first time. A truth as basic as the theory of relativity. And as potentially damaging as the effects of the depletion of the ozone layer in the atmosphere.

All the while, the Champ was unaware that a worried expression was building like a storm on his own face. And within that storm, in both eyes of it, you could see the seeds of doubt had been carefully and deeply sown, if you looked carefully.

And Alvin did look carefully, and when he did, he became even more relaxed, even more confident. Because, although the Champ did not know it, they were beginning an important battle. The climatic battle which would have a direct influence on who eventually won this war–the well-financed contest between himself and the Champ.

And the battle, a mental one pure and simple, was in fact, the ultimate key to victory. And it had started the very moment Alvin Thomas first opened his mouth in greeting.

Alvin knew that winning the battle–right then and there–might very well make the well-heralded war just an afterthought.

So, like a boxer throwing a series of body blows, Alvin now looked straight into the Champ's face to gauge the impact of each thought.

"Look, Champ. Shootin' for medals is one thing. But, when you're shootin' for money–and some of it's your own–you not only got somethin' to win, you got somethin' to lose," he said.

Like a chameleon, Alvin's face changed abruptly from an almost intimidating look to one of youthful enthusiasm.

"Anyway. That's what makes it fun–for me."

There is a special moment in every human's life. A moment when you discover that you are up against something so terrible, so utterly impossible, so decidedly one-sided that you need not even try. But you must. Because for whatever reason, you simply have no other choice.

And, that special moment arrived in the Champ's life the instant he heard Alvin so innocently utter the word "fun."

When he heard that fateful word, the Champ

painfully and inevitably turned toward Alvin, and like the proverbial Tar Baby, prepared to receive yet another blow.

"So, you uh, you like to shoot for money, huh? And, that's what you, uh, call fun?"

"Oh yeah. There's nothin' like it, and when I do, this strange feelin' comes over me. I've never been able to explain it."

Self-engrossed, the Champ described his own symptoms. "Kind of a tense feelin' all over?"

"Naw, just the opposite. The tougher the competition, and the more money I'm shootin' for, the calmer I feel."

The Champ still valiantly tried to act casual. "So you have shot for money before, huh?"

"Oh, well, just a few times when we had some contests back home. But of course, it wasn't the kinda shootin' we'll be doin' today."

The Champ blinked and for a second, just a second, looked a bit relieved. *Maybe there is a ray of hope*, he thought. *Maybe things aren't nearly as bad as they look.* Then he said brightly, "Oh?"

"Yeah. I had to shoot at movin' targets."

With things now every bit as bad as he had thought, and with all hope gone, the Champ sagged, and said quietly, "Oh."

Innocently and happily, Alvin continued on, "But that was a long time ago. Now I mostly just like to throw horseshoes–but, I still like to shoot."

Now the Champ's eyes started to show real,

gut-wrenching fear. He stammered, as he was barely able to spit out, "Then, uh, how come you didn't shoot in the regimental competition I just won?"

Alvin frowned and said disdainfully, "Oh hell, I don't care anything about medals. Not a thing." Then he quickly got back to the subject he wanted to talk about.

"Boy. That's a big responsibility you got, Champ. What with all your friends bettin' their hard earned money on you."

He pointed up ahead at the waiting group of soldiers, all now aware that the Champ and Alvin were nearly there.

"See 'em all up there? I'll bet they're all sayin' there's just no way you can lose. Yep. The kind of money they've been bettin' sure proves that they have faith in you. No sir! I sure wouldn't want a big responsibility like that!"

As Alvin and the Champ arrived at the rifle range, Durham watched closely as an anxious Wilkie greeted the contestants.

"Okay. Okay. You guys ready?"

Durham noticed the Champ looked a little out of sorts.

"You feelin' all right, Champ?"

The Champ said nothing.

Soldiers from all over the range had set their rifles aside, and walked over to form a ring around the Champ, Wilkie, Durham and Alvin. Some looked away to make sure no officer was watching.

Alvin cheerfully filled the void. "Here's my twenty-five hundred. Say, everybody else got their bets down?"

Heads nodded all around, as one soldier said, a little too loudly, "Hurry and get this thing over with, Champ. I got a 'Bama gal waitin' for me in town!"

When he heard everyone's laughter, Alvin's eyes narrowed as he made note of the general feeling that this would be a walk in the park for the Champ. He smiled almost imperceptibly. *Good!* He thought to himself.

Then, he spoke to the Champ, but really to everyone within earshot. "You know, this is gonna be fun, even though everybody here knows I don't have much of a chance."

One soldier smiled and whispered to another soldier, "Sure has changed his tune from last night."

The other soldier also smiled and added, "A canary sings real good 'til a big cat's got him by the throat."

Both contestants walked to the firing area, knelt on one knee, loaded their rifles, and prepared to fire.

It was Wilkie who decided the firing order, and said with a confident smile, "Okay, Thomas. Go ahead. Give the old Champ something to shoot at."

Wilkie waved at the target keeper, far down by the distant target.

Deep in a muddy trench behind the targets, a nervous private Taylor was being lorded over by tough, know-it-all, Sergeant Rutledge, who in a learned monotone, gave him the day's orders. "Today, your responsibility is the care and maintenance of the target area. There are men on the firing line, Private Taylor. Respond accordingly!"

Private Taylor quickly grasped a rope on a pulley and raised the target into view of the contestants. The job completed, he cupped his hands to his mouth, and yelled, "Fire–when–ready!"

At the firing area, the instant Alvin heard Taylor's distant voice, his eyes narrowed. The games were over. It was showtime.

Alvin took a quick glance at the Champ beside him, then he leveled his gun's sight on the distant target, and effortlessly fired four rapid shots.

Baam! Baam! Baam! Baam!

A long moment of silence was followed by the distant sound of Private Taylor's muffled voice from the target area, "Four–Dead–Center!"

At the target area, a disbelieving Private Taylor grabbed the target, and excitedly examined the four bullet holes, and the symmetrical pattern they had so neatly made in the bullseye. He marveled to himself, *Damn! Four dead center!*

Excitedly, he asked Sergeant Rutledge, "Who was that?"

Sergeant Rutledge, amused at the stupidity of the private's naive question, said sarcastically, "Four shots–dead center–and he says..." then he mimicked the private's amazed voice, "Who was that?"

With a pained expression, Sergeant Rutledge barked, "When you've been in this man's Army a little longer, you'll damn well know when the Champ's on the firing line. Givin' one of you greenhorns a little lesson, no doubt. Now get the next target up!"

Back at the firing line, the crowd of soldiers were thunderstruck, as they milled about, grumbling, unable to believe what they had just seen.

All except Wilkie and Durham. They said nothing. They made no movement. In fact, they exhibited no discernible signs of breathing. It was as if their shock had turned them to stone.

Unnoticed by all, Alvin delivered the coup de grâce to the Champ, in the form of a simple, yet coldly efficient whisper, "Damned glad I don't have a reputation to keep up, and somebody else's money on the line." Then he got up, walked a few steps away, and stood alone.

Once again, Private Taylor's muffled voice drifted up from the target area. "Fire–when–ready!"

Taylor's voice brought Wilkie out of shock. Defiantly, he said, "Okay. Show him what you're made of, Champ. Go get him!"

There was nothing but a stone cold silence. Absolutely nothing happened. The Champ appeared to be waiting for something.

Durham, finally reviving said, "You're the one, Champ. Now go ahead and get him, and get him good!"

But, still, nothing happened. Alvin stole a quick look at the petrified Champ, and smiled a small, knowing smile.

Durham could stand it no longer. Trying to act confident, he quietly told Wilkie, "I'd best go check things out." He quickly walked directly over to where the Champ appeared set and ready to fire. Bending down on one knee, then, looking around to make sure no one knew of his concern, Durham questioned quietly, "Everything all right, Champ?"

There was no answer.

Durham looked closely at the Champ and saw that his white knuckles were fixed in a death-grip on the rifle. He could almost hear the Champ's panicked heart, pounding wildly–Tha Thump–Tha Thump–Tha Thump–as he blinked and tried to focus his bug eyes on the target.

Weakly, Durham gamely tried again. "Champ. I said–is everything all right?"

Still no answer from the Champ.

Durham finally just took a deep breath, fixed

a gentle smile on his face and in a voice clothed in his best Doctor Kildaire manner, he said, "You know what I was just tellin' good old Sergeant Wilkie over there. I was sayin', I was sayin' that I'll just bet the old Champ has found himself in this kind of weird predicament many a time before, and this don't bother him, not even one iota. And I was right—wasn't I Champ?"

But, the Champ did not and, in fact, could not answer. For he had passed from this world—right on through the world of shock from where Wilkie and Durham had just returned—and entered another world, the totally debilitating, bottom-plumbing world of complete and utter despair.

His condition was evidenced by absolutely no discernible sign of breathing. In fact, the Champ looked exactly like a mummy. Soundless. Motionless. Frozen. And it was only when he noticed the telltale flood of sweat—which poured down the Champ's forehead and into his eyes—that Durham knew for sure that the Champ's internal organs were at least still weakly functioning.

But, inside the Champs's head, things were far from frozen. His mind projected a frightening story that only the Champ could see and hear. Demons borne of fear were loose. He heard their screams! Curses! They made the perfect soundtrack for the horror movie which was running over and over in his head, and carefully detailed every mistake he had ever made in his entire life.

No longer able to watch the pitiful sight of the Champ, Durham slowly got to his feet–deep in thought–and slowly walked back to the anxious Wilkie's side.

Fearing the worst but hoping for the best, Wilkie ventured, "So? What do you–uh, think?"

"What do–I think, Wilkie?" Durham said as he took a deep breath, then looked off into space searching for just the right words.

In a few painful moments, he slowly said with finality, "I think what we got here–is one scared little goldfish..." he nodded ruefully at the Champ, "... stuck in a jar, with one big damned shark." He nodded at Alvin.

Nearly in tears, Wilkie said, "...And we–we are backing that scared little goldfish?"

"One hundred and ten percent!" Durham said quietly and bitterly, as he cast his hateful eyes on Alvin.

A small, mischievous smile on Alvin's face and a twinkle in his eye signaled that he knew exactly what was about to happen.

Down in the target area, deep in the trench behind the targets, a wide-eyed Private Taylor was mystified. "What's the matter, Sarge? Nobody's shooting!"

"I know that you idiot! Most likely an equipment failure. Maybe a mechanical problem with the weapon's trigger," said Sergeant Rutledge.

"Want me to go see?" the private innocently

volunteered.

Rutledge blinked in disbelief. Then he forced a smile, shook his head, and said slowly, "Do I want you...you to go see?" He turned to Private Taylor and screamed, "Do I want the Kaiser for a roommate?"

He turned and started up the ladder, out of the trench. The higher he got the madder he got as he loosed his tirade at both the private and the situation. "Why this might require field stripping of the entire weapon! Isn't that the way it always is? Work with inexperienced personnel. End up having to do ever damned thing yourself!"

By the time he reached the top of the trench, Rutledge had talked himself into a stroke-inducingly blind rage as he stood, red-faced, hands on hips, glaring at the firing area.

Back on the firing line, the Champ was starting to revive, at least to the point he could hear more than the kettle drum Tha-Thump–Tha-Thump–Tha-Thump of his heart in his ears. As he looked down the barrel of his rifle, it appeared to him that the target had shrunk to the size of a pea. But now, he could make out a new target–and although it was blurred, it was bigger than a pea– much bigger–and it screamed to be noticed.

"Hey! I said hey up there! You'd better set your sights on the damn target and start some shootin!" Rutledge threatened.

Obediently, like a big gun on a battleship, the

Champ's gun slowly, mechanically moved, then stopped, aimed directly at Rutledge who issued a final, loud invitation, "Hey! Why don't you get off your ass and shoot?!"

So, more as a reflex than anything else, the robotish Champ obliged and his finger stiffly pulled off shot after shot after shot. The bullets and dust were flying around Sergeant Rutledge's feet as he moved like a bear in a shooting gallery, first to the left– Ping! – then to the right – Ping! – and then left again – Ping!

Finally, in desperation, Rutledge turned and frantically dove head-first, back into the muddy trench.

On the firing line, Wilkie, Durham and the others could only stand and shake their heads in disbelief.

At the target area, Rutledge–his face covered with mud–slowly peered over the edge of the trench and looked cautiously up at the firing line. Realizing the assault was finally over, he spat out some dirt, then disgustedly said, "Damn greenhorns!"

Later that afternoon, a soldier ran into the barracks waving a piece of paper screaming, "The war is over! It is over!" Everyone cheered and started a rough-house celebration–everyone except

Wilkie, Durham and the Champ. Wilkie and Durham leaned against a bunk where the Champ sat, and all three sullenly watched Alvin, sitting across the room on his bunk, industriously stuffing several bills in an envelope.

Durham was especially mad. "Damn! That's our money he's handling. Yours. Mine. And the Champ's."

"Was our money, you mean," said Wilkie. "And do me a favor." He nodded at the Champ. "Don't ever let me hear you call him, Champ, again!"

The Champ tried to defend himself. "He was just lucky."

"And I'm telling you–nobody–and I mean nobody, is that lucky," said Durham, defiantly in Alvin's direction.

Alvin heard him and walked directly over to them. "I'll tell you all one last thing. What I did today had to be skill–because I have never been lucky. If I was, I'd have had a chance to get over to Europe and help kick the Kaiser's butt!"

With that, Alvin Thomas went directly to the commissary where he mailed a letter to his mother, then found a table where he sat alone and started making plans for his future.

———————————

It was just before evening as Sarah Thomas

and the Preacher Harkrider sat on her front porch–
he on the highest of the three steps, and she in her
rocking chair. Alvin's old mule, Charlie, was still
hobbling around out in the yard, grazing aimlessly,
and going to fat now that there was no work to do
with his master gone for such a long time.

Charlie and the new Guernsey milk cow both
lived in a brand new, brightly painted red barn.
There was even a new bunch of plump chickens
next door in the hen house–noisy birds which
might have bothered Charlie in his younger days,
but now he mostly just ignored them, and their
loud, nervous clucking.

Behind Sarah and the preacher, the Thomas
house still stood, and stood better than it ever had.
It had been reinforced, after years of neglect, and
like the barn, it was also freshly painted–a bright
white–and now it was surrounded by a bed, full of
colorful, fall flowers.

The preacher was drinking all this in as he
listened to Sarah as she read from the latest letter
from her dear son, Alvin.

"... Also, I have discovered that there is plenty
of money out here in the world, and I want to make
sure you aren't in need of anything so I will
continue to send you more money as regular as
clock work. Your loving son, Alvin."

She took off her reading glasses, dabbed her
eyes and looked contentedly around her place. The
Preacher shook his head in satisfaction. He looked

down at a very old Ace, barely able to get around, yet still able to eat to his heart's content from his fancy new bowl.

Sarah appeared as if she had just come to a weighty decision. She looked seriously at the preacher and said, "I think you should encourage more of our young men to join up with the United States Army. They may be very surprised at how well it pays."

Chapter 6

On A Mission
In The Midwest.

It is an old saying that "nobody wins in a war"–
but that couldn't be said for Alvin Thomas. With
his substantial winnings which supplemented his
meager army pay, for the first time in his life, Alvin
had some real money. He wasn't rich, not even
close, but he felt like it as he started plying his
trade, living the life of a small time hustler, and
traveling across the heartland of America. Other
young men, some just back from the war, lived
the same kind of roving life, and lived it with more
bravado than brains.

But with Alvin, it was just the opposite. He
had the courage to try, but he also had his mother's
common sense and knew that although he had
already decided to go to New York City one day,
he wasn't ready yet.

The night he lost almost everything he had
in a poker game in Tulsa proved that. He'd been

dealt a full house, and felt good about it because he had won with less than that many times. But, he had never seen an opponent draw to a straight flush–and do it twice in one night. After that, he started to doubt if he had the kind of luck it took to win at cards on a regular basis. And after even more thought, he started to wonder if there might be more than luck to cards. If there was, he intended to find it out. Some way.

But he had a lot going for him. He was young, smart, had the gift of gab—but most of all, he would go to any length—-think and think and think as long as it took–until he figured out what it would take to win at whatever it was that someone else would bet he couldn't do.

Like the time in Tulsa when he had lost his bankroll–except for the twenty-dollar bill he kept hidden in his shoe–and couldn't afford to get into a card game. He sat in a rocker on the porch outside the hotel where he could only afford to stay one more night and rocked and thought and rocked and thought. Finally, he saw a farmer bringing in a load of peanuts, and he got an idea. The next day, he spoke a little too loud describing how the good Lord had given him an arm that was so sound, so strong, that it was almost the equivalent of a sling shot. The truth was–and he was willing to bet on it–he could easily hurl a peanut, clear over the top of the two-story hotel.

After considerable laughter, he had several

people willing to bet he was either crazy or had more money than he knew what to do with. So, with five hundred dollars on the line–which he did not have–Alvin looked high in the sky at the two-story structure in front of him, dramatically tested the wind with a moist finger, took careful aim, then reared back and let the peanut fly.

To the utter amazement of the assembled crowd, the peanut soared up–up–and easily over the building. When everyone arrived on the other side of the hotel, Alvin picked up the peanut and proudly showed it to the amazed losers, who after carping for an appropriate amount of time, paid off.

———————

A day later, on the train to the next town, Alvin had several hundred dollars in his pocket, and a lucky peanut to use when he needed it. He couldn't figure out why someone else hadn't ever thought of just filling a peanut shell with lead and tossing it over things to make money. *Damn*, he thought. *It's almost as heavy as a bullet and travels just about as fast.* The only tricky part was he had to make sure he was the first one who reached the peanut when it came down, so he could palm it and then show everyone a regular one. That was easy. The hard part had been thinking of the idea in the first place.

His conscience sure didn't bother him–not one bit. *And why should it?* he thought. The weight of the peanut had never been an issue. No one had asked and it was not his responsibility to volunteer any information. He had thrown the peanut over the building, just as he said he would, and that–was that.

———————

Surviving on the road wasn't always a question of outwitting people. Often, it was just raw talent and athletic skill that got him by. Traveling through the small towns of the Mid and Southwest, he won more than his share of turkey shoots and horseshoe throwing contests which were very popular and moderately profitable in some towns.

For a short while, he even joined a traveling medicine show, run by Colonel Adam Beaugardus, who hired him as the show's sharpshooting champion. He often said that Alvin was the best marksman he had ever seen–and he was.

That was the closest Alvin ever came to having a regular job with regular pay, but he finally decided it was not the kind of thing he could do on a regular basis. He had now learned that it was the excitement of not knowing what would happen the next day that got him out of bed each morning. So, to the deep regret of Colonel Beaugardus, Alvin left the show.

Just as the ducks knew when it was time to leave the Ozarks each fall for the south, one day, for a couple of reasons, Alvin just knew it was time to head on to New York.

Not only had he seen and learned enough about gambling and working his propositions, but he had also seen another young man who had his own special peanut, and was working the very same proposition Alvin had perfected just a couple of years before. It would have been bad enough if Alvin had started to repeat himself, but seeing someone else do it for him was the final proof he needed that it was high time to close the curtain on his small town days.

So, he sat down and wrote his mother about his decision, and then went right out and bought a used jalopy–not good enough to impress anyone– but plenty good enough to get him to where he was headed.

———————

Preacher Harkrider made it a habit to hand deliver the latest letter that Alvin had written his mother. He was especially glad he had brought the one he had delivered that day.

There was big news. *Must be*, he thought. She had already started crying.

"So, where does your Alvin say he's headed?"

"Says he's finally off to New York. New York City."

She ducked her head, covering her face in her apron. The preacher heard her gentle sobs.

"Now, sister Sarah. I may not be as experienced as some in the ways of the world, but I have been all the way to St. Jo–and I don't reckon that New York City is much bigger, or much tougher than that. Couldn't be. So, yes Ma'am. I do believe that your Alvin is ready for New York City."

She raised her head, smiled through her tears, and said, "Oh, I'm not worried about that, Preacher. I just hope New York City is ready for my Alvin!"

Years later, Alvin would fondly recall that it was on that first trip to New York City that he actually swung a golf club for the very first time.

He had been driving his old jalopy down the narrow, two-lane road which connected St. Louis and Kansas City, when he noticed by the side of the dusty road a crudely handwritten sign which read:

Golfing Can Be Done Here
3 Complete Holes
25¢

He passed the sign and traveled a hundred yards or so, then slammed on his brakes and backed up to the little road which the sign marked. He turned onto the road that was little more than a cow path and ended near a shed on which hung another sign reading:

Golfing Shop

Alvin got out of his car, and with the look of a young man who had decided to try something different, he walked over to a counter covered with old, dirty, badly-cut golf balls, and several well-worn golf clubs.

Behind the counter, an attendant slept peacefully, so Alvin took a moment to look around his very first "golf course." It was little more than exposed rock, dirt and small, occasional patches of green grass where cows contentedly grazed.

Two older men, both dressed in farm overalls and work boots, putted their balls on a brown patch of dead grass masquerading as a putting green.

This all looked intriguing to Alvin who tapped on the counter and woke up the sleeping attendant, a man who should have had better things to do, but didn't. He managed to get up and walk over to Alvin.

"I've heard about this game. Mostly for rich folks, huh?" said Alvin.

"Not here it ain't. If you got twenty-five cents,

some golf clubs and a ball or two, you can play all day if you want, rich or not."

Alvin fished out a quarter from his pocket exposing a roll of bills. The attendant noticed.

"If I did decide to take this game up, I expect to do pretty good, so I might be wanting to buy some of these golfing sticks."

The attendant, smelling a possible sale for the first time in a long, long time, opened a small closet, and brought out a brand new set of golf clubs.

"Are you in luck! I only got one set of clubs for sale, but you're just gonna love 'em."

Alvin looked at them closely–all shiny and brand spanking new–and said, "Oh, I see. You get the metal ones and the wooden ones too, huh?"

"Yeah. Today you get them both! Kind of a special deal, you know? *Stay calm*, the attendant thought. *You may unload these clubs yet. Don't let this rube get away.* "Use the woods when you're a long ways from the hole–and use those irons when you're closer."

"The irons–yeah–I got it. And the woods. Okay. I'll just try them out."

"Fine." He handed Alvin a basket full of balls.

"Uh, so where do I hit them?"

"Anywhere you want." He decided to try a new sales technique he had just read about. "Say, here's one of my brand new balls to get you started on the right foot."

Alvin walked over to an open area, shooed a couple of cows away, selected the driver, and as he did, he watched the two men putting on the "green." He shifted his grip, trying to do it exactly as they did.

Something was wrong.

He turned to the attendant and said, "Hey! My clubs aren't working like theirs! Mine are backwards!"

"Just turn your body around the other way. Do everything backwards. It'll all work out!" *Damn!* the attendant thought. *Even this hick knows those lefthanded clubs aren't worth a shit!*

With a shrug, Alvin just turned around, readjusted his hands and said, "See what you mean." He teed up the new, white ball, took the club back and swung as hard as he could–and whether it was beginner's luck, or simply a natural athlete finding the best part of his best sport–the ball he hit that day roared off into the distance–with neither a hook nor a fade–and it did not come to rest until it had traveled precisely three hundred yards.

The exact distance of Alvin Thomas's very first drive was never a matter of conjecture, since the attendant and the two men dressed in work clothes all walked the distance off in utter amazement, three separate times.

When he returned, the attendant noticed Alvin had already put the set of clubs back on the counter and was headed over to his car. Stunned at what he had seen, and desperate to sell the clubs, he called after him, "Hey! I will make you a great deal on these clubs!"

Alvin got into his car and started the motor.

The attendant panicked. He had a natural lefthander, right here–right now–who could hit the ball out of sight, and he was getting away. "Come on! You got to buy 'em," he begged. "They were made for you!"

With a smile, Alvin said, "Well, I wouldn't know about that. Got important business in New York City. Anyway, I can't see myself wasting my time, chasing a white ball around a cow pasture."

How stupid does he think I am? Alvin thought as he drove away. *No sir! I'm too smart for that!*

Years later, Alvin would laugh when he remembered what he had told that attendant, never realizing how wrong that statement would prove to be–in every possible way.

Chapter 7

A Little Mint
for That Julep?

Seven years later, in the early morning mist of that spring day in 1927, the Long Island Country Club looked like a stand-in for "Tara," the plantation right out of *Gone With The Wind*.

The imposing white structure stood high on a hill and hid–very exclusively–among oak trees. Somehow, you sensed even the oaks had been carefully screened before they were allowed to grow in this private domain.

Down from the main building, a winding road unraveled until it reached the main entrance gate on which a small, discreet sign read:

LONG ISLAND COUNTRY CLUB

MEMBERS ONLY

Outside the club's golf shop, it was already a

busy time. The clatter of golfers' spikes on cement signaled the arrival of the early birds, those gung-ho golfers who considered a weekend day wasted if it wasn't started on the course and as early as possible.

Inside the golf shop, the chatter and general hubbub of the very rich sounded like assault troops as they prepared to attack the golf course.

From a sea of Gatsby-like faces, words floated up such as *"Stock market"*– *"New Bentley"*– *"Fired my chauffeur"*– *"Sticky divorce."*

Even ahead of this enthusiastic group–out on the first tee box–stood two anxious young caddies, Hank and Little Bob. Hank was older and knew the ropes on this golf course. Little Bob was smaller, younger and obviously new to all this. And, he appeared nervous.

Hank took a look at his uneasy cohort, and decided to give him a positive thought to begin the day. "Your very first day and you're gonna see Titanic play. Don't happen very often."

Little Bob didn't have a clue as to what he was getting at. "Titanic? You mean like the ship? What kind of name is that?"

"The perfect name for a guy who sinks everybody who bets against him. Big winner. Big tips. Guaranteed!"

Little Bob thought he got it. "Great golfer, huh?"

Hank, with a knowing smile said, "Well–he sure knows how to bet."

"He a member here?"

"Naw. He has people who owe him–rich folks–and they can get him on any course he wants. But he don't play anywhere regular. Moves around so nobody gets used to his game–or his face."

Little Bob was confused. "Why?"

" 'Cause he–aww hell. You'll see. Look. Here he comes."

Hank pointed at a man in his early-thirties, who was striding confidently toward them and the first tee box, with a set of golf clubs over his shoulder.

"Titanic," as Hank had called him, was none other than an older Alvin Thomas with a nickname. His friends just called him, "Ti." And the years had been good to him. Very good indeed.

He appeared slender, taller than most, and moved with that special grace of a natural athlete.

But the one, most striking thing about him was, and always had been, his eyes. They seemed to enjoy a hint of danger and bored right through you.

Just before Alvin reached Hank and Little Bob, Woodcock, a nervous country club member, intercepted him and said nervously, "Ti, okay. I fixed it up. You're my guest for the day. Now this will buy me some time to pay off my gambling debts to you, right?"

"Sure will."

"But going into the nineteenth hole or the club house is not part of the deal."

Ti had heard this all before, and smiled through the indignity as he said, "No problem. That's the way it works at all the country clubs I play."

Woodcock suddenly had a panicked second thought. "Oh God! You're not playing against any of our members, are you?"

Ti gave him a look of total disdain as he answered curtly, "No chance."

A relieved Woodcock brightly said, "Great! Then go skin them."

Ti smiled faintly. *Sure,* he thought. *As long as it's not your ass.*

Woodcock carefully looked around to make sure no one had seen them talking, then ducked his head and sneaked away like a thief in the night. Ti turned and stepped to the first tee where Hank and Little Bob waited.

Hank quickly developed a case of nerves and was almost beside himself, as he fumbled to take the golf bag Ti was carrying.

"Morning. Ready to go, men?" Ti said cheerfully as he extended his hand in greeting.

Totally losing it, Hank dropped Ti's clubs and extended his hand with a huge smile.

"Yes, sir." He proudly pointed at his chest with his thumb, "I'm Hank, and I'll guarantee that

I'll take good care of you today, Titanic, and–"

Suddenly, Hank froze in mid-sentence. He closed his eyes in utter despair. He had just broken a sacred vow–one that every caddy who ever was fortunate enough to work for Ti, had taken. Right off the bat, he had made a big mistake. He tried to recover. "Uh, damn...I mean...I mean Mister Thomas."

Ti waited a painful moment for the lesson to sink in, then he carefully explained, "Now that's a good point. It's worth a lot to me–maybe a whole lot–for you to forget Titanic today. If anyone wants to know, I am Alvin Thomas, from Rogers, Arkansas. Every time. Okay?"

Hank was repentant, and flustered. "You bet. Sorry. It's Mister Thomas. Every time. Every time anyone says anything I'll be sure and..."

Ti knew the lesson had been learned, so he smiled and let him off the hook with, "Okay. Good enough."

He turned to the other young caddy, who had been drinking this show in with absolutely no idea of what was going on, and said, "And you are..?"

Little Bob was awed, but still managed to look Ti straight in the eye, as he said with as much conviction as he could muster. "Little Bob. I'm Little Bob."

Ti smiled at his bravado. "Okay then, okay, Bob. Same thing goes for you."

Little Bob never expected to be treated with

any respect from his peers, much less from this mysterious man, who so intimidated the older caddy. So, it was with genuine respect that he said, "Yes sir, Mister Thomas."

At that moment, from behind the two caddies, an older, heavy-set man, George McGuire, approached–out of breath and running late.

Little Bob hurried over and took his golf bag as George stumbled up to the tee box.

Ti had a look of mild frustration as he said, "Hello, George. You're late."

Ti walked over to George, who was mopping his brow–still trying to catch his breath–as Hank quietly updated Little Bob. "That's George McGuire. He's Ti's pal on and off the golf course."

"Can he play?" asked Little Bob.

"Like an old man. But a nice guy and he tips pretty good, too."

Meanwhile, George was updating Ti. "Okay, we're up against two guys from Cincinnati–lotta bucks!" George looked over Ti's shoulder and saw two men heading their way.

"Damn! Here they come already. Anyway. Pretty good players."

Ti noted their approach and asked quickly, "Do they know about me?"

"Not from what I hear. You're just Alvin Thomas from Rogers, Arkansas. Unless someone tells them different."

George looked over at the caddies. "Do you

think they...?"

Ti smiled and winked at the caddies.

"Got it covered, George."

The two men, Gus and Milburn, arrived, smiled, and extended their hands in greeting. Two caddies also accompanied them and carried their golf bags.

It was George who handled the social formalities, "We're all a little late. So, what say let's tee off and I'll introduce everyone as we play." He nodded at Milburn and Gus. "You guys go ahead."

Everyone nodded at the time-saving idea. Gus and Milburn quickly pulled their drivers from their bags and began to loosen up with practice swings.

George decided to test the waters. "Actually, we don't normally play for money, but if you want to make a little bet, let's talk about it after the first hole."

As first Gus, and then Milburn, teed off, Ti leaned closer to George and whispered quietly through clinched teeth, "We don't normally play for money? Where in the hell did you get that one?"

George was flustered, but answered quietly, "Shit, I don't know. Just popped out. I was running late–had a flat. Grabbed a taxi." He looked at Ti pleadingly. "Can I get a ride home?"

"Sure. Whatever, George. But, you've got to start planning a little better."

"Ti, nobody plans the way you do."

Ti suddenly sniffed like there was an aroma. Still whispering he said, "Smell that, George?"

George looked puzzled. "Smell what?"

"Cincinnati money."

Then Ti really went to work. He carefully studied the golf swings of the competition.

Gus was a huge, bearish man. He swung his driver with brute force and hit the ball a ton. Ti could tell he always hit the ball a long, long way– if not always straight.

But Milburn was a different case study entirely. A small, thin man, he was not very long off the tee, not long at all. But, he was very careful. He almost guided his ball–begging it into the fairway–and he was always straight, but never long. And, he was, quite obviously, the brains of this twosome.

When it came George's turn to hit his drive, he was, as always, true to form. Not very long, and not very straight.

When Ti addressed his ball, Gus and Milburn noticed he was lefthanded.

Ti swung his driver smoothly, and hit it straight. Not as far as big Gus. But dead straight.

As they all walked down the first fairway, Ti casually fell in step with Gus and Milburn as he said, "Damn, Gus! You hit the ball out of sight."

Gus smiled and offered Ti a cigarette. With a shake of his head, Ti refused and continued, "I've been thinking. You two not knowing the course and all, I don't think it's fair for us to even make a small wager, which is what I was about to offer–just to keep things interesting."

Milburn eyed Gus. "Wager" was a word they had used before.

He gave Gus a cigarette, they both lit up and inhaled deeply. Trying too hard to act casual, Gus said, "Well, if you think a bet would make it more interesting, then by all means, let's do play for a small one–just to keep things interesting."

"Oh. Couldn't do that," Ti said. "You both being from out of town and not knowing the course. I have a motto–George does too."

George looked at Ti. A motto was news to him.

"No sir," Ti continued–as if he was reciting a poem. "If it's not fair for you–it's not something we'll do."

Milburn almost hurt, he wanted to bet so much. He tried to keep a poker face as he said, "Well, then, what bet... would be fair?"

Ti thought for a moment, then said sincerely, "We wouldn't play you for one red cent, unless one of you gentlemen, like you Gus, was allowed to take three full swings off the tee on every hole–except par threes of course."

Milburn blinked. *Is this Christmas? Or have I died and gone to Heaven?* he thought.

He took a drag on his cigarette, stalling, so as not to appear too anxious; then he slowly answered, "Well now, that–that seems imminently fair to me."

Milburn eyed Gus and nodded his head ever so slightly. Their secret signal–get the bets up.

Gus went into action. Trying to sound innocent, he said, "How–uh–how much would you gentlemen care to wager?"

Ti was all smiles–Mister Congeniality–as he smiled and said, "On the occasions we do wager– and this appears to be one of them–we always go along with whatever is comfortable. You gentlemen name it."

Gus and Milburn quickly huddled, spoke intently for a few seconds, then Milburn turned back to Ti and said, "My partner gets three swings off every tee box–except par threes. Correct?"

Ti nodded.

Milburn took one last look at his partner, another drag on his cigarette, then as calmly as possible said, "Well, what about–what about one thousand dollars?"

Seemingly stunned, Ti blinked. But then he recovered and said, "Wheew! That is pretty steep, boys. Pretty steep! But okay. What the hell! A thousand dollars a hole it is!"

Now it was Gus and Milburn's turn to be stunned. Recovering, they were barely able to control their joy. Although it was springtime, both Gus and Milburn would have sworn they heard the jingle of Christmas bells. What they had been after was only one thousand dollars, and now the odds were good–very good–that with Gus's three extra swings on many of the holes before them–and any luck at all–this might be a huge payday. A day they would remember for a long time to come.

And the truth was, it would be exactly that kind of day.

All the while, George had watched and listened. Now, he was seriously worried and he walked over to Ti to try and get an explanation as to what was going on–but Ti moved away. He did not want to talk right now and George knew that he was at his partner's mercy.

So, George and Ti watched as Gus and Milburn went to work, just as earnestly and industriously as a couple of prospectors about to mine pure gold.

The bets started on the third tee box, where Milburn swung first, and hit his drive straight–but not far. Then Gus confidently and joyously swung, and swung, and swung, as each of his three drives went further than the last.

The next hole, the result was exactly the same. George was not even a factor. And though Ti easily outdistanced Milburn by thirty yards, it made no difference. It was big Gus who easily outdistanced George and Ti, and with his extra distance and extra swings, he appeared a cinch to win every hole after that for his team.

And so it went as the holes slid by. The

Cincinnati boys quickly and easily won not only the 3rd and 4th, but also the 5th, 6th, 7th and 8th holes, and the star of each tee box was the carefree, ecstatic Gus, who happily swung, and swung, and swung–like a gleeful whirling dervish.

It was on the 8th green that a disgusted Ti slammed the flag in the hole, then turned to the smiling Gus and whined, "Damn! That's six thousand dollars we've lost."

Milburn had his pencil in hand and was figuring his team's winnings, when he heard Ti say, "Milburn. How about giving us a chance to win a little back?"

Even though things were certainly going their way, Milburn was–if nothing else–a cautious man. He carefully answered, noncommittally, "How so?"

A frustrated Ti said almost pleadingly, "If we could just raise the bet to–oh hell, I don't know–how about two thousand a hole–and if we got lucky–which sure isn't likely with the way old Gus is smoking that tee ball–well, it might at least give us a sporting chance."

Milburn quickly answered, "That would be fine," as he almost pushed Gus to the tee box and said even more quickly, "Hit, Gus!"

Gus's first drive sailed way out there–like the many he had hit before.

George looked even more worried than Little Bob and Hank were confused. This whole thing made no sense. No sense at all. Here was Ti, blundering into one bad bet after another, and no one could figure out why. It appeared he had simply just lost his senses.

But, right then–right at that exact instant–something happened. Something that neither George, nor Hank, nor Little Bob–and certainly not Milburn or Gus–ever imagined would happen. For at that moment, Gus hit his second drive on that 9th hole, but–it did not quite explode off the driver as had the others before.

But worse than that–at least for Milburn and Gus–the third drive just barely lifted off in flight, and made it a scant one hundred yards down the fairway, before plunging to earth like a dying quail.

Yet, Milburn barely took notice, and hit his ball, as always, one hundred and seventy-five yards, straight down the middle.

With a knowing look, Ti quickly and effortlessly hit his drive also straight down the middle, but every bit of two hundred and seventy-five yards. About twenty yards past Gus's longest drive.

A frightened, nervous Gus moved over to Milburn's side and spoke quietly and confidentially to him. "I got a problem. A big one!"

Milburn thought his partner was kidding and said with a smile, "We've already won six thousand dollars. What problem could you possibly have?"

"The problem of not being able to swing

anymore."

As proof, he tried to raise a match to light a cigarette. His hand shook so much he couldn't. Big Gus was terrified, suddenly submissive as he continued, "See, I've got no strength left! My arms–my arms feel dead!"

Milburn's eyes darted from Gus–to Ti–back to Gus–then finally back to Ti.

Milburn blinked. Then, he shook his head trying to clear the cobwebs and maybe dislodge the thought he was having–a totally frightening thought–which was consuming his mind as he watched his partner–only seconds ago so powerfully potent–now hopelessly helpless.

"Gus, you don't suppose..." He lowered his voice. "You don't suppose–Thomas is a hustler, do you?"

They both turned, shocked at the very thought, and stared at Ti, who chose that moment to look away at something which had caught his eye–something flying high above them on that beautiful spring day.

It was a formation of Canadian geese, and Ti watched–enthralled–as they held a tight formation, and etched an almost perfect V in the bright blue sky.

By the time the golfers reached the fourteenth tee, Milburn was reduced to desperately pushing–sometimes pulling–Gus up to each tee box, like they were finishing a death march.

George, Hank and Little Bob were finally relaxed, but Ti–the game no longer afoot–was getting bored. And boredom was something he simply could not stand. It was like poison to him. So, desperate for something to interest him, he surveyed the life of the idle rich as it existed up, down and around the idyllic fourteenth tee box, at the prestigious Long Island Country Club.

He saw–behind the tee box–a lake which stretched out as far as the eye could see, and he watched as a college rowing team glided by.

Elegantly attired couples strolled among the willows, growing lakeside–and on the shore was a small, discreet, free-standing sign which read:

Caution! No diving! Shallow lake!

Amidst all this, Ti was suddenly aware of a small commotion. It was the sound of flashbulbs popping as cameras caught a dashing young man, Jack St. James, posing as if he had just swung his golf club. Jack was about Ti's age. He was blonde, handsome and had a blinding smile.

Ti noted the way Jack enjoyed the excess, in fact, seemed to thrive on it. Then, something else suddenly caught his attention–a beautiful woman– who was also being photographed with St. James. A brunette, she appeared to be in her early twenties, and not only did she catch Ti's attention, but she held it.

And little wonder. Alice Reed was one of those rare women who, although beautiful, was not taken with herself–not looking for another mirror in which to see herself. Instead, her eyes were bright, her mind inquisitive, and she was always on the alert to see the best in everything and everybody.

As the beautiful couple smiled for the cameras, two *New York Times* reporters, Dale Turner and Patrick Ivins, waved their arms–pencils and paper in hand–desperate to ask a question of Jack.

Turner, a heavy-set man, who sweated as a matter of habit on even the coldest day, called out, "Jack! Need a quote for the morning edition. So, how does it feel to be called, the finest golfer on the East coast?"

Jack smiled, and paused for a second as he brought up from memory, his prearranged and carefully worded statement. "It is an honor for which I have worked extremely hard–and so yes, I am grateful–and no–I certainly do not take that sort of acclaim lightly. No–far from it..."

Turner quietly whispered to Ivins, next to him, "Shit. I should have just asked him to read us something really interesting–like the phone book."

Ivins smiled to hide his disgust and whispered, "God! What an onerous jerk!"

As Jack waxed on and on, Alice noticed Ti was looking at her, and it didn't bother her one bit. In fact she returned his gaze gladly, and for a long while. Alice was neither bashful, nor someone who scared easily.

Then, just as fast as it had arrived there at lakeside by the fourteenth tee box, the public relations junket with Jack St. James in the lead, headed for another location, sweeping Alice along with it.

In the Club's parking lot that evening, as Ti and George got into Ti's car–a sporty, nickel blue roadster–Hank and Little Bob finished loading the golf clubs in the trunk.

His job done, Little Bob walked around the car to George's window. George leaned out, and with a smile said, "Thanks, son." And with that, he casually put a bill in the young man's hand.

Little Bob's eyes lit up. "Wow! Five bucks. Thanks Mister McGuire!"

Expectantly, a smiling Hank walked around to Ti's window on the driver's side.

Ti leaned out and said, "Hank. How much did you make caddying here all day yesterday?"

"Almost two bucks."

Ti nodded and then handed Hank two, one-dollar bills.

"There you go."

Hank looked disappointed. In fact, crushed.

But Ti wasn't through, as he asked casually, "And–what's my name?"

A dejected Hank could barely speak as he stared at the measly, two dollar bills still in his hand.

"All day long it was Mister Thomas."

With a smile, Ti handed him a fifty dollar bill. Hank could only stare in disbelief. He was utterly speechless having never seen such a large bill.

"Good thinking, Hank. And the lesson is, it pays to have a good memory."

"Yes sir, Mr. Thomas! And, thank you. Thank you very much!"

Hank and Little Bob walked away, still staring at their money, as Ti started the car and pulled out of the driveway of the club.

As the roadster sped away in the distance, Gus and Milburn stepped from behind a pillar, followed by an interested Gerald St. James, Jack's father.

Gerald St. James was an older man–gray-haired and distinguished looking–who was always dressed precisely in a suit and tie, and always walked with a cane.

Gus tried desperately to lift one arm to point at Ti's departing car–but sadly, the big man simply could not. The rigors had set in. Gerald noticed that Gus's arms simply hung uselessly at his side.

A fuming Milburn had to point for Gus and

as he did, he said, heatedly to St. James, "Is Thomas one of your members?"

St. James was indignant. "Absolutely not! And on behalf of the membership of our club, I would like to express our deepest apology for your losses."

That bit of public relations seemed to soothe the ruffled feelings of Milburn, at least for the moment. "Well anyway, it certainly wasn't your fault, Mr. St. James."

"Please, please. Call me Gerald."

"Of course, Gerald, and thank you for cashing my personal check."

"Our pleasure–and although I must rush home for a business dinner, I do hope you will give all my best wishes to all of our many friends at your fine golf club in Cincinnati."

Milburn ate up the flattery, like so many crispy donuts, and wholeheartedly accepted Gerald's apology with a warm hand shake and smile. After helping Gus to do the same, they both walked away to lick their wounds in the 19th hole.

But it was Gerald who had learned something that day, for he stood there for a long moment, squinting into the evening sun to watch Ti's car fading into the distance. Intrigued, he smiled, and simply said quietly to himself, "So, that's Titanic."

Ti and George were miles away and speeding

down the highway, when George opened the glove box, took out a .45 revolver and casually handed it to Ti, who put it into his leg-holster.

Ti slipped a diamond ring on each of his hands as George counted their winnings and handed Ti his share.

George shrugged and said, "Fourteen grand, less my twenty percent. Pretty good day."

"But not a Howard Hughes day," Ti said as he looked quickly and intensely at George.

George blinked like a boxer who had been punched once too often. He smiled weakly. *Oh God, please! Not Howard Hughes again*, he thought. He quickly tried to change the subject.

"So, Ti. How did you know old Gus would give out like that?"

"Big guy–big swinger like Gus–he's got maybe twenty ball-busting tee shots in him in one day. That's all. After that, he's real average–kind of pussy whipped." He looked over at George. "Learned that when I was a kid. Boy–did I learn that."

George looked puzzled. "You didn't play golf when you were a kid."

"No, but after working my mule, lifting logs all day, I could barely lift a tin cup to my lips. Same with over-swinging a golf club."

George laughed as he realized that–as always–Ti had been way ahead of him. In fact, he had been way ahead of everyone all day.

George confidently summed up the whole day with, "So, Gus's goose was cooked after the eighth hole, right?"

In a sharp, serious tone, Ti countered to make an important point.

"No! Gus's goose was cooked on the second hole–when Milburn got greedy. How many times have I told you, George? I don't do anything to anybody. They do it to themselves. And it generally has to do with either fear or greed–especially greed. Yep. When I see greed–and I usually do–I see a real opportunity."

George was suddenly serious.

"Ti. If you'd had to–could you have beaten old Gus without hustling him? You know–with no tricks?"

Ti laughed and said, "Sure. I was just having a little fun today–and doing a little business."

Then he sensed that there was more to that question than he first realized.

"Why, George?"

"Because I think the day is nearly here when you'll have to prove you are as good a golfer as you are a hustler."

Ti was cautiously optimistic–unusual for him–as he said, "I'll be ready–when the stakes are high enough."

Suddenly, a light flashed across Ti's brain. "You mean Leo Flynn is finally going to get me into some big-money match games?"

"Ti. You have a chance. But, we still have to convince him. The good news is he says he'll listen, so head on to Lindy's–he gets there about now."

Ti hit the accelerator pedal, hard. This was what he had been waiting for–and, of course, a match with Howard Hughes.

Uncharacteristically ahead of Ti, George wanted to clear something up right then and right there. And he did. "But Ti he can't–I repeat–he can not get you a game with Howard Hughes."

The name Howard Hughes was like comfort food to Ti.

"Keep working on it, George."

In frustration, he repeated what George had heard so many times before.

"Can you believe? Hughes offers to play some guy a little golf for a million dollars–a million dollars–and the guy turns him down?"

In a wistful voice, he said softly, almost longingly, "Damn. I wish I'd been there."

Ti was like a kid as he repeated what had become his mantra, "Win a million dollars–and I can join a country club and walk in the front door with the other millionaires."

———————

Later, at Lindy's, the one New York restaurant where the elite actually did meet to eat, Ti and George sat at a table with Leo Flynn, golfing promoter for the coming big money matches.

One look at Flynn and you knew that he'd been around–and so had his rumpled suit.

Like the fighters he had promoted and managed, Flynn pulled no punches. He casually stirred his drink, and spoke to George–but nodded at Ti, like a side of beef. "Don't need your boy, here–George. I already got one. Billy Ford."

Then he looked coldly at Ti, and actually spoke to him. "I hear you do some pretty clever stunts and you're a good bettor–a real good bettor. But I take golf serious–like I did boxing when I managed Dempsey."

George was getting worried. This was not a good start. "But Ti can play, Leo."

Flynn was not impressed. "Maybe. Maybe not. I got a world-class reputation. Can't risk that on a–a circus act," he said, almost with disdain.

George fumed. Ti's eyes hardened, but he stayed calm, and with a glance, urged George to do the same.

And their rapport was not lost on Flynn, who casually added, "Notice I didn't say–cheap hustler."

The Irish in George erupted as he jumped up and threw his chair aside, ready to fight. "That's it! Put 'em up."

Flynn was neither impressed nor frightened by the outburst. He never even moved, except to simply continue stirring his drink.

His attitude made George even madder. "Why you sonofabitch! I ought to..."

Ti held George back and then with a smile, he said calmly, "George. Can't you see Mister Flynn is just trying to burn my ass? Seeing if I can take it?" George gathered himself and slowly sat down.

Now Flynn was impressed. He took a close look at Ti and confided, "If you're out trying to make a twenty foot putt on one of those country club courses, and some blue blood says your shoe ain't tied according to Hoyle–I don't want no player of mine crying all the way home. I want you rock-solid. Tough."

He pointed at his own arm. "Not here!"

Then he pointed at his head. "Here!"

He leaned closer to Ti and warmed to his subject. "Lot of talent out there on those golf courses. Lots of it. The guy who's got it between the ears and behind the eyes..."

He looked at Ti's cold, piercing eyes.

"He's the guy who's going to bring home the bacon. And that's all I'm after. Not the blue ribbons."

George smelled a sale. "Look, Flynn. When you get those big match games set up on those swank country club courses, it's Ti here you'll need playing for you."

A thought crossed George's mind. He looked at Flynn closely. "Say, how much are the blue bloods willing to wager on their club champs? We talking big money?"

Flynn's eyes shifted uncomfortably. His business was his and nobody else's. But he knew he had pushed them far enough. He had done his research and heard enough about Ti's reputation for carving up the competition on golf courses to know he deserved a chance. It was just a business deal now, and he hated to leave anything on the table if he didn't have to.

So, rather than put them in their place, he just played it casual. "Aww. It's hard to tell."

But Ti was like a dog on point. He sniffed the air and said, "Smell that George?"

George seemed confused. "What? Do I smell–what?"

"Bacon. Lots of it."

Then Ti quickly turned to Flynn and in a cold, steady voice, said, "Leo. Let me play. I'll win."

Flynn liked that approach, but he still needed to see just a little more hunger in his potential associate. "Like I say. Got a boy. Billy Ford. Good player. Just don't need you to play."

"Then let me play Ford. I'll beat him. Then I'll win all the big money matches for you."

Ti waited a few seconds for all this to sink in. And since this might be the only time he could carve anything extra out of this deal, he took a chance and said, "That is–if I can make side bets on myself."

Intrigued, but not wanting to show it, Flynn swizzled his stick in his drink for a long moment and bought precious time. Time for him to figure out just what in the hell he was going to do. He weighed everything very carefully. Then, in his own, very deliberate way, he announced the sum of his thinking, in his matter-of-fact tone.

"If you did beat Billy–which you won't–and I did take you to the big money matches–which I'm not promising–you'd get all the action you wanted because you–you would be a big underdog."

Flynn had made up his mind and got up to leave. "And that–might be interesting."

Ti and George leaned forward in their chairs. They hoped that this was going to be one of those really big moments in a lifetime.

And it was.

Casually, Flynn made an announcement. "Ti. You and Billy. Two o'clock tomorrow. I'll let you know where."

And that was it. With no more fanfare than ordering extra dressing for a salad, at a restaurant table in New York City, the biggest match of Ti's life was on.

Chapter 8

Will The Winner
Please Step Forward–
Please!

Two o'clock P.M. had seemed like it would never arrive, so Ti had occupied part of his time by reading the society section of *The New York Times*– something he normally didn't do. But–he found what he was looking for.

Right on the front page was a smiling Jack St. James, directly beneath a headline which screamed: Noted East Coast Golfer Ready for Action. And on the left hand side of the photo, barely in frame, was the beautiful brunette he had seen the day before.

And he finally found–buried far down in the story, as if it had been included only as an afterthought, what he had really been looking for. The brunette's name: Alice Reed.

He cut the photo out, stuck it in his wallet, and as he drove with George to the Palmetto Golf

Course–not a fancy layout like Long Island Country Club where he had played the day before, but still, a challenging one–he had to work to get Alice Reed's beautiful face out of his mind.

But, if there was one thing Ti could do, it was totally focus on just what he had to do, at exactly the time he had to do it.

So, when he arrived at the first tee, Alice Reed was safely tucked away in his billfold and his memory where she would not interfere with the business of the day–Billy Ford.

Only George, Flynn and a few casual onlookers stood around the first tee as Ti and Ford shook hands precisely at 1:58 P.M. However, one member of the press was there, as always, eating peanuts and appearing to be only casually interested. Ti smiled and noted that it was Turner, the same reporter who had so reluctantly covered the St. James photo shoot the day before.

Ti carefully studied his opponent, quickly measuring the fact that although Ford was not tall, he looked strong and was well-proportioned for golf. And, he had a well-earned, solid reputation for hitting the ball from tee to green as well as anyone around.

A quick coin flip had given Ford the honors, and with little fanfare, he quickly teed up his ball and sent a rocket down the heart of the fairway–well out there.

Ti did the same.

Any knowledgeable onlooker would have immediately concluded that there didn't seem to be as much as a particle of difference in the two men's abilities.

The first hole was halved with pars. The second with birdies–after Ti effortlessly recovered from a bunker–and the third was also halved, again with birdies, with Ford having to make a putt from well over 30 feet.

And, he did.

So it went with Ford and Ti both hitting shot after shot and tying hole after hole. Both players knew it was a death match, and the resolve on their faces reflected the realization that they knew only one would move up to the new, higher arena.

While this normally makes for great drama, as well as a great match, in this case–at least in Leo Flynn's mind–it did not.

With every splat of an iron–with every thwaaak of a wood shot–Flynn became more and more sullen. George accompanied him around the course and noticed that he was not a happy man. And, if there was anyone in the world that George and Ti needed to be happy– at least on that day–it was Leo Flynn.

So, George decided to strike up some good-natured banter and ventured, "Nobody could ask for a better match, right Leo?"

Flynn looked at him with disdain. "Hell, I could!"

George realized he had said exactly the wrong thing. One look at Flynn's sour face–now getting redder by the second–and he could see that he had done the equivalent of bringing up Howard Hughes's name to Ti.

He smiled weakly, prepared for an onslaught, and said innocently, "Oh?"

"Well, shit yes, Georgie! Look! I need someone to step out and take this thing. Take it by the teeth–shake it–and eat it. Eat it right up!"

George had seen anger before, but not like this. The longer Flynn talked, the angrier and redder his face became.

"The worst thing that could happen would be for these two to end up in a tie!" He turned his head toward heaven. "God! Spare me! Please! Not a damn tie! They've played twelve holes and I'm looking at a possible damn tie. I'm a businessman. I can't afford to flip a coin. I need a decision! I need a winner!"

Even though Flynn and George were far enough away from the players that they weren't being disturbed, George knew he had to break this up. It could lead to no good.

George decided to do what had worked earlier with Ti, when he was on his Howard Hughes tirade. He would simply change the subject. So, he quickly and confidently said with a little extra bravado, "Well hell, Leo. At least you're lucky to be out here in this fresh air!"

The look on Flynn's face at that moment was pure hatred, as he said, "First of all, standing around a boxing ring is bad enough with all the smoke and crappy air–I've got a terrible sinus condition, you know–but now, I get into this damn golf matchmaking business, and I'm stuck out here in the damn pollen and mold–hell I can't breathe– and my sinuses are draining–damn near bleeding to death–and on top of that I got two guys playing like they're kissing their sisters–and you've got the nerve to tell me that I couldn't ask for a better match? And that I'm lucky to be here where I can die in this beautiful air!?"

A few inches from George's terrified face, as was his habit–Leo summed it all up. "Georgie. I need a winner, damn it! I need a damn winner!"

And maybe–just maybe–as a tribute to such an incredible outpouring of pure negative emotion, God took pity and actually did answer Flynn's desperate plea. Because at that precise moment, Ti hit what appeared to be yet another wonderful shot–except–that an almost inexplicably strong gust of wind came seemingly from nowhere, swept his ball up, and pushed it far to the limits of the left fairway, where it bounced twice, hit a small rock, and then careened at a strange angle, straight toward a huge oak tree–directly in back of which the ball finally came to rest.

In short. Ti had no shot. No shot at all. And, when Flynn saw the situation–while wishing Ti no ill–he simply said, "Bad luck. That could hurt."

Ford also carefully noted Ti's position, but said nothing. He watched intently as Ti walked over to his ball, studied it carefully, then took a long look at the immense oak tree directly in his path to the green. To even see the green Ti had to walk around the tree, so he did, looking back at the ball again almost in disbelief.

Ti's caddy shook his head. Things–including his projected tip–were suddenly not looking good. Not good at all.

The proverbial hush actually did fall over that small crowd watching that important match at Palmetto golf course that day. Trouble–especially the kind a golfer finds–has a way of silencing almost everyone. And this silence was screaming that there might just finally be a winner after all, and this might be the moment when he would emerge.

As everyone looked at Ford, who so confidently waited for Ti to make his play, the thought crossed Flynn's mind that Ford would make a good choice for him after all. In fact, he'd probably been right to choose him in the first place. He'd been in the sports business long enough to know exactly how to put the right spin on any athlete he promoted. And how to justify, even to himself, that choice.

On the other hand, George was thinking in a different pattern. He figured that if they had blown this golden opportunity–and every indication was that they had–Ti would increase his obsessive campaign for his long-awaited chance at Hughes. So George was thinking that maybe a trip to California where Hughes lived might now be the next order of the day.

But of all the people there that day, the one person who looked the least worried, strangely enough, was Ti.

In fact, as he approached his ball with the club he had chosen, a small smile escaped his lips.

Then he said, quietly, almost casually to his caddy, "You know, son. Sometimes you just have to remember–this is only a game."

And with that, he took his stance and addressed the ball. Then, in seemingly less time than a heartbeat, he took his wood back–back–and then through the ball as he calmly smooth-stroked the most beautiful fade known to God or man, sending his ball fading right around the tree in front of him–then over the creek guarding the front of the thirteenth green and up onto the green, where the ball rolled and then finally came to rest only twelve feet from the pin.

But, as miraculous as Ti's shot had been, Ford and the rest of those gathered there saw that the ball had come to rest above the hole, at the top of what appeared to be virtually a hill. Ti would be faced with a desperately hard, downhill putt from that precipice.

Not worried, Ford shrugged and, from his position in the middle of the thirteenth fairway, hit his ball straight and long, to within a mere ten feet of the pin–directly beneath the hole.

He smiled as he approached the green and gave his putt a closer look. He liked what he saw. Just ten feet. Straight uphill. Now he knew he finally had Ti by the balls. He couldn't help but smile again, as he spotted his ball with a coin and stood aside, as Ti lined up his putt.

From his vantage point high above the hole, Ti looked his putt over carefully. Then, almost to himself, but just loud enough for his caddy to hear, he said, "This thing is going to break twice. First–soft and kind of gentle to the left–then, quick and down and dirty to the right."

Over by Ford's ball, his caddy, helping him line up his putt, said, "This one's as straight as a turkey ever went to shit."

He pointed at Ti's ball. "Glad you don't have his. Im...possible."

Ford nodded, smiled slightly, then said in a relaxed voice, "Yeah. He's finally in trouble."

But just then, something totally unexpected happened. Something that Ford had never experienced before. And Ti probably knew that– maybe even counted on it–for he said brightly, loud enough for all to hear, "Hey Billy! What say you and I put a little something on these putts?"

Ford was totally shocked. He was unable to

even think for a moment, but finally blurted out, "Well, I...uhh...I..."

Then Ti said, "Well, hell, Billy. I'm not talking about much–just a couple a hundred."

Chapter 9

And...
The Legend
Starts to Grow.

The peanut eating reporter, Turner, dominated a table at Clancey's Speakeasy as he recounted the events of the day to his enthralled audience, comprised of fellow reporter, Ivins, and several bar patrons.

Turner held his hands to the sides of his face in disbelief as he said, "... And today, right there on the thirteenth hole, I witnessed the single most competitive moment of golf I've ever seen."

He paused for effect, as he took a big gulp from his mug of beer, "And I've seen a lot."

Ivins could barely stand it. "What? What was it? Who hit what kind of shot?"

He ignored the question. "That moment was, of course, the defining moment of the match."

Then he turned to the other reporter. "And it wasn't any kind of shot, Ivins. It was what Ti said."

He took another gulp and then set about to get the story out and straight. "Picture this. Titanic's looking at a twelve–maybe thirteen-foot putt–a downhill speed putt mind you–that has two breaks, maybe a third. Ford's putt is easy. A cinch. And Ti has the balls to say to Ford, 'We don't have to bet much. Couple a hundred is fine with me.' "

Ivins and the others around the table didn't get it. One man says, "So? How much did Ford bet?"

Turner just smiled and waited patiently. He was ready to spring the trap. To teach a lesson in competition. To define the illusive and seldom-seen "defining moment." "Ahh. That's just it. Gentlemen, he bet nothing. Absolutely nothing. Not one red cent. Not a farthing. Not a guinea. Not a peso. Not a..."

"Okay. Okay. Nothing! Nada! Got it! So, what happened?" begged Ivins.

Turner just smiled a wonderfully silly smile–just kept looking down at his glass–dragging that wonderful moment of center stage on and on, until he finally explained, "Gentlemen, Ford just quietly said, 'Uh...I guess I'll pass on that, Ti.' "

He took another drink in silence. Ivins was lost. "Wait a minute! That's it?– 'I'll pass'–that's all he said! Big deal!" Ivins complained.

"Big deal is right. Ti makes his putt. Billy three putts, loses the hole. Then loses the next three after that. It was all over. Ti closed him out–four down, two to play–on the sixteenth."

The onlookers still didn't get it, so Turner continued, "See? Ti had him dead to rights the moment Ford was afraid to bet. It's Ti with the double-breaking downhill speed-putt, but it's Ford who's intimidated. Totally. Ti knew that he would make his putt. But more important, Ford did, too."

He took another drink, draining his glass, and motioned for a refill. "See the poetry in it?" He looked around the table at the slack-jawed audience. "Aw, probably not. But at least you can understand that–damn! Now that was a match! An important one too, because it means Ti will play for Flynn in those big money–country club match games."

Something suddenly struck him. "Say. Anybody got a list of who is playing for who in those matches?"

Ivins reached into his coat pocket. "Yeah. Got it this morning."

Turner took the list from Ivins and studied it carefully, running his finger carefully down the long list–reading each contestant's name aloud to himself, "French, playing for Meadowbrook. Callahan, playing for Grassy Sprain. Ti shouldn't have any trouble with these guys..."

But then he stopped, took a drink, and nodded. "Uh oh. Here's a good one. Jack St. James. Let's see, he'll be playing for Long Island Country Club."

Ivins looked puzzled. "Can't get a handle on that St. James guy."

"Who can," said Turner.

"The best player on the East coast, they say? And, if he wins the Transcontinental in Florida, next he'll be called the best player in the country. Seems like he needs a little better test than that," said Ivins skeptically.

"If he plays Titanic–he'll get it!"

Everyone laughed.

———————————

That night, outside a downtown movie theater, Ti walked up to the ticket booth and said to an attractive young woman working there, "One, please."

On the wall of the theater's entry way, he noticed a poster advertising the feature now playing. It read:

Her passion could not be satisfied.
His devotion could not be measured.
Together they looked for...

LOVE IN A QUIET PLACE.

Starring:
Beatrice LaMont
and

Gerald Abney!

A sign was glued at an angle across the bottom of the ad which read:

LAST DAY!

The young female ticket taker was obviously taken with Ti. She said demurely, "Only one?" and smiled seductively.

As she handed him his ticket, he looked at her intently, then moved a little closer. She did too. He smiled. She did too. Then he asked her the question he was aching to ask her. "Say, any chance Howard Hughes made this movie?"

"I wouldn't know," she said, crestfallen.

Ti turned and walked into the theater. In the flickering theater light, he seated himself–and soon, the long day of golf having taken its toll, he dozed off.

Moments later, Alice Reed wandered down the aisle next to him, searching for a seat. She spotted one next to the sleeping Ti, eased by him, and sat down, all the while, keeping her eyes glued on the screen.

She immediately started to read the subtitles of the silent movie–and she read them aloud. "I don't care what you think, darling. That's the way it will be. Surely you must feel my poor heart pounding."

From behind, a disgruntled patron tried to quiet her with, "Shhhhh!"

Alice, totally absorbed, continued. "Hush! Hush! My darling!"

"That's a good idea. Hush!" another patron said.

Someone else jumped in with, "Yeah. Hush!"

Oblivious to the criticism, Alice continued reading. "Can't you see that the maid can hear every word we're saying. Don't worry, my dear. I'll take care of the maid. Ruth! Please leave."

Another bothered patron chimed in, "That's more like it. Leave!"

"Do you think I mind? Ha! I'm sick of this place."

Just then, Ti woke up and heard Alice speaking aloud. From her words and dramatic tone, he naturally assumed she was speaking to him, as she said, "Do you hear me? I'm sick! Sick! Sick!"

"You okay, Ma'am?"

Alice continued to look at the screen as she leaned toward Ti to hear him better. "Oh, I hope so. What do you think?"

Ti was confused. He stared at the emoting Alice, and even in the dark, he recognized her as Jack St. James's beautiful photo-mate. But, he couldn't figure out what was going on. "What?"

"How do I look? Do I look all right?"

Ti looked at her face very closely. "It's just too dark in here to tell. But if you feel bad–I'll call a doctor."

Alice turned and looked closely at the man next to her for the first time. She recognized him too and remembered their visual encounter at Long Island Country Club.

She pointed up at the screen. "No! I mean up there. Do I look all right up there?"

Ti turned to the screen and saw Alice on it. She was Ruth, the maid in the film.

Not fishing for a compliment, just wanting an honest opinion, she asked, "Look, I know it's hard to tell. They put so much makeup on you, and all but..."

The disgruntled patron behind Alice leaned forward, tapped her not-too-gently on the shoulder, and said, "Lady, if you can't be quiet. I'm gonna..."

But, whatever he was going to threaten to do became a moot point as Ti straightened up in his chair, turned slowly around and fixed an icy stare on the man. "The lady's doing her work. Practicing her trade. Any problem with that?"

The man cowered and slunk back, deep into his seat. "None at all, pal. None at all."

Alice saw and heard it all, and then added, in an effort to cool things down, "Thanks, but you can both relax. I'm leaving."

She leaned over and whispered to Ti, "My part is nearly over anyway."

Alice reached for her purse which she had laid on the floor, and as she picked it up, the purse's edge hooked Ti's pant leg and accidentally pulled it up. Looking down, she saw Ti's .45, tied to his leg. She was shocked.

Ti continued looking at Alice up there on the big screen, unaware of what she had just discovered.

Alice thought for a second. Then, more than a bit curious–and always looking at the positive side of things–decided to venture a guess as she looked closely at Ti. "Police?"

Ti looked around quickly. "Where?"

Alice realized she had guessed wrong. "Oh. Never mind."

As Ti turned back to the screen to again watch her, Alice took the opportunity to really study him closely. Even in the flickering light she could see his diamond rings. *No. I guess not*, she thought.

Then, she whispered brightly to Ti, "Excuse me, please." He quickly stood up, let her pass, and sat back down, as Alice proceeded up the aisle toward the lobby.

But Ti quickly decided not to waste this unexpected opportunity, so he got up abruptly and followed her.

Alice walked through the lobby and waved to Charlie, a man working behind the candy counter.

Charlie gave her the high sign and said, "Gonna be in any more movies, Alice?"

"I'm working on that right now." Then she

breezily walked out the front door calling out over her shoulder, "And to all a good night, Charlie."

Charlie looked after her a long moment. He liked that girl. And this was not lost on Ti who made it a point to walk over to Charlie's counter, "How about some popcorn, Charlie."

Charlie grabbed a bag and handed it to Ti, who slapped a dollar bill down on the counter.

"See you around Charlie."

Charlie got the point as Ti hurried to catch up with Alice.

For awhile, he was content to just follow and watch her as she seemed to glide down that dark New York City street. He was a long way from Arkansas, and on rare nights like this one with a woman as beautiful as Alice in sight, he wondered if he couldn't take a little more time away from his golfing and gambling obsessions for a little fun.

Maybe he had earned the time it would take to have a little more enjoyment with the opposite sex. But work was all he knew. All he had ever known ever since he left Arkansas. Sure. There had been women, but they were just a matter of convenience and necessity. Nothing serious. But, this girl was different. *What the hell*, he thought.

He caught up with Alice and said with a smile, "Need a ride? I'll get us a cab."

"No thanks. I'm just going down the block," she said.

"Then, mind if I walk with you?"

Alice turned to refuse. But, seeing his face clearly for the first time that night, she quickly changed her mind. She had worked with some pretty handsome actors, but this guy, *Wow*! she thought. In a split second–her mind racing–she mentally categorized him like another actor on a call sheet for a movie.

Dark eyes–check that–make it mysterious dark eyes. Dark hair. Six feet tall–check that–make it six foot-one. Slender. But not too slender. All in all, just about right, she thought. Yes, she decided, he was just right for most any call list for a leading man. But, after the gun in the holster, maybe he wasn't right for her personal call list. *Still*, she thought. *I can't just keep working with no chance to meet anyone other than Jack St. James. He's rich. Good looking. But–God! He is so full of it. And himself. So, I'll take a chance. I'll at least walk down the street with this guy. After all. Why not!*

Her complete analysis and decision took less than a fraction of a second. Such is the way of nature.

Then, she answered his question, "No. Not a bit. Mister...?"

"Thomas. Alvin Thomas. They call me Ti."

It's a good fable that men and women should "meet cute" in stories, as if that is what always happens in life. "Meeting cute" means that the couple will be more interesting, first to each other, and eventually to the audience, if when they meet, there is conflict–initial distrust and/or problems. All of that makes for the emotional fodder–the complications, which the couple must overcome in the story, so that by the last Act, all is forgiven, and all problems have been worked out. But "meeting cute" was not the way it happened on that dark night in New York City. Instead, there was an instant attraction between those two, and, as they strolled down the sidewalk both eating Ti's popcorn, they wondered about each other's past, present and future, because they were genuinely interested in–and attracted to–each other.

"So, you're in the movies?" he said.

"Barely."

Ti looked puzzled, so she explained, "Look, I only got that part on the screen tonight because they were shooting here in New York."

"They don't do that a lot, huh?"

"They used to. But now they film mostly in California."

Ti again looked puzzled.

"Something about the weather. Too cold in New York to shoot outside year 'round. Warm on the coast. Probably gets down to money. Money. That's what the movie business is all about."

"Most businesses are."

Alice couldn't argue that logic. "Good point."

"Well anyway, looks like easy work."

Alice's eyes flashed. "Easy! Ha! The work is

hard, very hard. And even harder to get."

"So, how do you get it? Just walk in and say–give me a job?"

"No. Sometimes I crawl." Alice smiled. *Where did this guy come from?* she thought. "Ti, everyone wants a job in the moving pictures–any job! I was just lucky."

Ti took careful note of that part of Alice which surfaced at that moment. He liked that part. The feistiness. It fit well with the other parts. The vibrant beauty. The quick, determined mind–the–well, when he thought about it, he really hadn't found any parts of her's–mental or physical–that he didn't like. They all fit. And fit well.

"Someday the moving pictures will have sound. Imagine, you'll actually be able to hear the actors' voices!" she said in amazement.

"From where I was sitting in there tonight, you already could," he said with a smile.

Like George, Alice knew when it was time to change the subject. "Well now, Mr. Thomas. What do you do for a living?"

"I live off my wits, mainly."

Alice didn't understand.

Seeing that, Ti fleshed it out a little more. "I deal in sporting propositions–like golf."

She smiled and nodded, but it was obvious to Ti that she was still lost.

"Alice. I'll do nearly anything that I know for sure I can do, that somebody else–for some reason–is damn sure I can't."

He waited for the light of recognition to go off in her eyes. It did not. "Alice. I gamble!"

He gambles? she thought. *That's it? That's all? God! I thought he might be a gangster. A murderer. But–the gun! What about that gun down there?*

So, with these unanswered questions in her mind, she decided to buy a little more thinking time with an old actor's ploy. The shocked response. The personal affront.

With the back of her hand raised to the side of her mouth like Lillian Gish, she exclaimed in a Southern damsel's drawl, "Gamble! Did you actually say gamble, sir! Then I must inform you, Mr. Thomas, I was raised not to consort with men who engage in games of chance."

Ti liked the act, and remembered his mother's earlier warning. He smiled and repeated aloud what he had vowed to himself so many years ago, "Then there's no problem, Alice. When I gamble, nobody's got a chance but me."

That did it. In one fell swoop, he had both upstaged her and won her over–as he heard her say warmly, "Ahhh, a bit of a shark, huh?"

She looked at him for a long moment. "Sounds like you don't like to lose."

"Who does? The trick is not to give the other guy a chance to win."

"And how do you do that?"

"It's not easy. But I usually figure a way."

"So, you like money?"

"I like to win. Money's just the way I keep score."

"Well, it looks like you've been scoring rather well. Now I understand why you have..." She pointed down toward where she had seen the gun on his leg–"It!"

"Does–it–bother you?"

"Nothing bothers me since I left Pittsburgh." She had a terrible thought. "Have you ever–have you ever had to use..." again she pointed at his leg, "...it...on anyone?"

"You mean kill somebody?"

Alice's eyes were as wide as saucers as she nodded.

"Only when somebody tried to take something from me that wasn't theirs."

A frightened Alice was now in so deep she was actually getting scared, but she had to know the answer. "Uhhh–how–uhhh–how many men have tried to take–uh–"

Ti interrupted to save her the pain. "Four. Not proud of it, Alice. But most of them were wanted by the law anyway."

"They were?"

"It's a fact. Another fact is, the police almost congratulated me last time. Even gave me a permit to carry–" he pointed, as she had, to his leg, "...It."

Alice smiled. She was greatly relieved. "So,

you're not a gangster. You're..."

"Just in a dangerous profession. But I gotta admit, sometimes I get pretty close to the edge."

"What keeps you from going over?"

"Don't have to. I'm too good. It's the ones who aren't who have to cheat–trying to keep up."

"Hmmmm." She smiled. "The confident type."

"You gotta feel good about yourself–if you're gonna be a winner."

They came to a corner and Alice nodded at a building. "This is it."

Ti looked up to see the ornate entrance of The Plaza Hotel. He was impressed. "So, you live here, huh?"

"Oh, I'm in and out so much, it's hard to tell."

"Guess I'll be saying good night, then."

"Good night."

As Alice turned and walked inside, Ti watched her intently. He called after her, "You do work hard, don't you?"

She gladly turned back to him. "Yes, I do. And the harder I work, the luckier I get."

"Yeah, I like that, Alice." He winked. "I sure like that!"

Alice nodded, then added quickly for no reason other than she was afraid she might never see him again, "Call me?"

He smiled and tipped his hat, "Oh, you can bet on that, Alice. Good night."

"Yes–it was," she said quietly to herself as she watched Ti walk away down the dark street. Then she entered the front door of The Plaza Hotel and disappeared inside.

Alice went directly to Frank, the front desk clerk. He smiled and showed her two messages, both of which he had already read, which was his habit in case she just phoned in as she often did.

As he handed the messages, one at a time to her, he previewed each for her. "Your laundry is ready. And, here's one from that old rascal, Jack St. James. Says he'll pick you up at ten in the morning for golf."

Of all the guys in the city, why does she go out with that jerk? he wondered.

Chapter 10

Jack Be Nimble,
Jack's a Prick.

The next day Ti pulled his convertible over and parked in front of The Plaza. He cut the motor, jumped jauntily out, and was headed toward the hotel's entrance when a familiar voice rang out. "Hello Ti," said Alice, from where she sat in the front seat of another roadster, parked just a few feet ahead of Ti's car.

Ti walked over to the car and saw that Alice was sitting next to none-other-than Jack St. James. He was dressed in a brightly checkered sweater with a white collar exposed, matching checkered socks, knickers, golfing cap, and he affectedly puffed on an ornate, English pipe, with the St. James family crest carved on it.

As Ti leaned over to talk to Alice, he noticed a set of golf clubs in the rumble seat. He tipped his hat to her and said, "Alice, I was just coming to see you."

"How nice," she said as she turned to Jack. "Oh, Mr. Thomas, I'd like to introduce Mr. Jack St. James."

Ti and Jack barely nodded at each other. But, it was St. James who, after quickly sizing Ti up, said, "Well, as you can see...it was Thomas, wasn't it?"

He answered his own question with, "Whatever," and started again. "Well, Thomas. As you can see, we're off to spend a day at the golf course. So if you'll excuse us, we'll just be on our way."

Ti was in no hurry to see Alice head off with Jack, so he leaned further into the car and, to the obvious dismay of Jack, made himself comfortable, leaning on the door sill. Then casually, slowly, he started a conversation with Alice. "So, you play golf, huh?"

"Oh no, not me. I just watch. But Jack is really very good."

"That a fact?"

Jack gunned his motor, hoping that Ti would take the hint. He didn't. So, Jack smiled insincerely and said, "Actually, a man is only as good as the equipment he uses. Speaking of equipment, by Jove, I can hardly wait to unsheathe my new driver again. Gad! What a club!"

As Jack's phony British accent echoed in his ears, Ti continued to watch Alice. Jack was well aware, as he said, "I'd venture to say that one of my drives yesterday must have gone two hundred and sixty yards."

Ti and Alice were still looking at each other as Jack, desperate to interject something that would get a response said, "You do play golf, don't you, Thomas?"

Ti didn't have to be asked twice and quickly said, "Is that an invitation?"

"Well, uh–of course."

"Then, let's go tee 'em up!"

———————————

At almost four o'clock that afternoon, on the fourteenth tee box at Long Island Country Club, almost at the exact spot where Ti and Alice had first set eyes on each other, Ti looked as though he was about to jump out of his skin. And he was, because he was in the worst of all conditions for him. He was bored. Almost bored to death.

All I wanted was to spend some time with Alice, he thought. *And here I am stuck, nurse maiding her date. Damn!*

He quickly tired of watching Jack waggle his new driver affectedly in front of Alice, who was trying to act interested, so Ti began watching the beautiful people on the most beautiful hole on the Long Island course.

He watched a couple wading far out in the shallow lake. Another couple shared a picnic lunch which they had spread out beneath the shade of a willow tree growing on the bank of the lake a few yards from the tee box.

As Jack spoke a little too loudly, Ti was drawn back to the moment and his eyes locked on the two objects of Jack's affection. First Alice, and then that damn driver.

Jack saw that Ti had finally noticed his prized golf club, and almost shoved it in Ti's face, as if he had begged to see it more closely.

Then Jack said, "This is the latest, the ultimate driver. Give it a feel old chap. But–do be ever so careful."

He ceremoniously handed it to a disinterested Ti, who waggled it a few times as if testing it, as Jack continued, "The pro who sold it to me assured me there will never be a driver that will hit the ball further than mine! Never! It's made from Peruvian wood–laboriously selected from only prime, virgin forests, then cut and slowly aged in thatched huts in the deepest recesses of the Peruvian jungle, a minimum of five humid years– makes it impervious to moisture don't you see– then, it is floated by canoe, down-river to an old man–arguably the finest primitive wood artist in the world–who with his very own, stone-ground axe, hand carves each and every driver head. Only five in the whole world. Four were sold to royalty in Europe, and this..." he pointed at the driver as if it were the Holy Grail, "This is the only one west of St. Andrews."

Ti had heard far more than enough. "No offense, Jack. And I have to admit, you hit some real ball busters today–but I always say it's the man that's using the driver that makes the difference. I kind of like my old driver," Ti said as he patted his own, store-bought driver as affectionately as if it were his old dog, Ace.

With a calculating smile, Jack said, "Thomas, I haven't seen you out there, nearly as far as me off the tee, all day."

Ti was getting a little hot, and although he prided himself in keeping his temper–because he knew losing it was the fastest way to lose any money he might be betting–this was in front of Alice. *This is different*, he thought as he eyed Jack coldly and muttered between clinched teeth, "I like to pace myself."

Jack was many things–arrogant, shallow, vain–but not stupid. And he quickly saw that he finally had Ti's interest, even if it had been earned by dredging it up along with some anger. So, with a measured amount of satisfaction, he continued, "We all have our excuses. Some are better than others."

Ti's eyes flashed. His face turned red. He was livid! Alice guessed that his anger apparently had overcome him, for his words spilled out like a stream of consciousness flood.

Ti pointed at Jack and said, "Not right now–

but using my old driver–if I had time to work out–get stronger–get on some good vitamins–in about six months–in about six months, St. James–if the wind was right and I got a real good bounce–yeah in probably about six months–from this spot right here on the fourteenth tee at your own damn country club–I could drive a golf ball–Jack–I could drive a golf ball five hundred yards!"

There was nothing but stone cold silence for a long, excruciatingly painful moment. Then Jack laughed hysterically.

Even Alice was shocked. "That's a long way–golf wise–isn't it, Ti?"

St. James was still laughing and gasping for breath, as he finally blurted out, "That's...the length...the length of five football fields!" He smiled smugly at Alice. Then he looked incredulously at Ti and said, "And you're sure? Absolutely sure you can do that very thing?"

Without waiting even a second, Ti retorted, "Sure enough to bet you any amount of money you name!"

"Any amount?" Jack repeated in disbelief. "Thomas, if I thought you were serious, I'd take your money."

Ti said with finality, "I can do it. I will do it. And I repeat, I'll bet as much as you want! In fact, I'll even give you a whole month to decide!"

By the time they reached the eighteenth green, things had finally settled down a bit. At least it appeared that way to Alice, as she watched Ti and Jack both carefully studying their final putts of the long day. But after the ruckus on the fourteenth tee box, she was confused. *Five hundred yards! My God! What was Ti thinking about?* she kept asking herself. *Maybe Jack will forget all about it.*

And, she had seen another side of Ti and was very uncomfortable with it. She knew that anger like that had to be controlled, or it could be debilitating. Destructive.

Ti seemed to have slipped into a sullen mode when–after reading his own twenty-foot putt, and deciding how hard and exactly where to putt his ball–he watched, irritated, as St. James laboriously studied, and restudied, and studied even again, his relatively simple, ten-foot, straight-in putt.

Ti could stand the boredom no longer as he sarcastically said, "St. James! It's not that I haven't enjoyed the beauty of your course and the peacefulness of the round–but don't you think we ought to put just a little action on the table?"

Jack's face was blank, as Ti continued, "Put just a little excitement in the day?" Jack still didn't get it, so Ti spelled it out. "Look. We're all even. This is the last hole." He waited for the light to go off in Jack's brain, but it did not. "I'm sorry I didn't bring a trophy we could play for, so how about making some kind of bet on these putts? Come on, Jack? It's our last chance of the day."

"Well, if you put it that way, maybe a wager is in order. Fine. Yes, fine then. What about twenty dollars?"

Ti just smiled. "I was thinking about something a little more interesting. I was thinking– how about this? The winner takes Alice home, and not only that, but the loser can't see her–or even talk to her–for a whole month?"

"Oh, no, no, no! Absolutely not!" Jack said, as he noticed some of his country club "friends" had gathered around the green.

Some had tennis racquets. Others were in swimming attire. But all of them had overheard the bet Ti had voiced, and they loved it, and mischievously told Jack so. "Come on Jack, old boy," one said. Another quickly added, "Ten feet! Child's play. My Auntie Katherine could make that one. In fact, she did just yesterday!"

Everyone laughed loudly. Even one attractive, very shapely, young woman got into the act and said, "Oh, come on, Jack. Don't be such a chicken!" To the delight of the group, her date even did a near-perfect imitation of a chicken clucking.

Jack tried his best to neither accept, nor offend, as he turned to the assembled crowd of "friends" and said, as diplomatically as possible, "I certainly would accept that bet, but, Alice would never–absolutely never–lower herself to be an idiotic prize in a stupid bet such as Thomas envisions."

Alice stole a look at Ti, then turned to St. James. "Jack. I do consider myself a prize. So, sure. Come on. Sounds like fun," she said, amused.

Though taken aback, Jack finally nodded his puzzled agreement, and said, "Uh–well, very well then, Thomas. The winner has Alice to himself for one full month."

With a wary eye on Ti, St. James said, for all to hear, with a bit too much bravado, "Thomas, I do believe you are away."

Ti nodded, took a quick look at Alice, and smiled knowingly. He walked directly up to his ball, coldly took one last look at his target, and routinely knocked his ball into the dead center of the hole.

The crowd of Jack's amazed friends were abuzz, as they moved about and watched as Ti picked up his ball from the hole, then joined Alice to await Jack's putt.

The crowd noticed with pride, their old friend, Jack. Yes, their Jack, who simply leaned so elegantly, and so motionlessly on his putter–while maintaining that stoic, half-smile which was frozen so bravely on his face.

They knew that in doing this, and doing it so very perfectly, Jack again was displaying the carefully cultivated St. James tradition of total self-composure. Yes, the knowing crowd had seen it before–but maybe, never before had they seen it done so well. Yes, this was definitely the ultimate display of St. James disdain, which Jack was directing at Ti's just-made putt.

As they watched Jack standing there so stoically, they never dreamed the truth. For the truth was that Jack did nothing but stand there–simply because he could not do anything else. His body was frozen in shock. But his mind wasn't. It was racing wildly. *Shiiiittt!!!!!* his mind screamed. *Oh, Shit! Shit! Shit! I have to make this putt–just to tie! I cannot win! There's no way to win!!! But– I must at least tie. I must!*

Then, mercifully–all emotion drained from within–Jack was finally able to move. He swallowed hard and stole a glance at Alice, who was trying hard not to look too happy that Ti had already holed his putt.

As Jack's friends decided to root him on, with "Atta, boy!"–"Go get him, Jacko"–and, "Into the hole, old chum," Jack could barely breathe as he tried to go through the ritual of lining up his putt. All the while, high above him on the club's second floor portico which overlooked him and the eighteenth green, his father, Gerald, sipped his drink and watched his son's total disintegration below.

Another club member, Arthur Tipton, walked out on the balcony and joined Gerald. He smiled and watched the action below.

Jack crouched nervously over his putt, and squeezed his putter until his knuckles were white. *Which way does that grain run?* he wondered as he tried to breathe. *Could run to the left and straight to the lake–but–that slight breeze out of the south–it might balance that and move it back to the right–and whoa, hold on. Looks like it might be a little uphill–or maybe it's slightly downhill. Hmmmmm–Oh shiiitttt!!!!! Shit! Shit! Shiiiittt!*

Finally, Jack managed to stand over his putt, take his putter back, and then through the ball, which started off in the general direction of the hole.

Above, Gerald watched sadly as Jack's ball– well off line–did not even come close to the hole and sped far past it. Gerald shook his head in deep disappointment as Arthur casually commented, "Well, looks like someone just got beat!"

Deep in thought, Gerald answered pointedly, "Someone just got murdered."

There was a certain look on Gerald's face. A resentful look that said this controlling father sensed a growing problem. One he might have to deal with personally.

———————

That evening in the club's parking lot, Jack tried to keep up a good face as he helped Alice into Ti's car, closed the door and said anxiously,

"Don't worry, Alice. I'll see you in a month. One short month."

Jack smiled weakly and watched Ti and Alice driving happily away.

———————————

It was after dark when Ti and Alice arrived at The Plaza, and Ti said, "How about some dinner and dancing?"

"Fine."

"Then, I'll be back to get you in an hour."

A worried look appeared on Alice's face. "Maybe an hour and a half?"

"Sure," he said as he started to get out to open her door.

"Ti, don't bother," she said as she looked up. "Looks like rain. See you in a bit."

As Ti drove off, Alice entered The Plaza and went directly to Frank who was reading a newspaper. He saw Alice headed toward him and reached for her messages.

"Hello Frank, I'm in a big hurry."

"You got quite a few–don't know if they are important or not," he said.

As she carefully scanned each message, Frank watched her admiringly and smiled. He liked this girl. Everyone did. Honest. Bright. And most of all, trustworthy. He didn't mind taking her calls, he'd do it for free–and had offered. But he knew she didn't want to put upon him or rather–to be in his debt, even though he had become a good friend to her.

She had taken his advice and discovered it to be sound. A lot of girls she had met since she came to New York–far too many–had started out trying to make it as an actress, but in a pinch, had been forced to take too many "gifts" from men, and had not only never made it as an actress, but ended up working in another profession all together. The oldest one. Or, being kept. At least for awhile–until her "benefactor" thought she was too old or, out of boredom, simply found someone else. Then one day, she found her clothes and belongings out on the street, from where she had come.

No, Frank knew he didn't have to worry about Alice. She knew that when a man offered her a "helping hand," he did it–more often than not–with the expectation of "helping himself." No, as tough as it was, she thought of herself as a startup business, undercapitalized for sure, but with a bright future, as long as she didn't make that one, big, fatal mistake now.

Finishing her messages, Alice quickly looked around to make sure no one was listening, then lowered her voice and said, "Frank, I know I owe you for taking my calls, but–"

Frank knew where this was going, so he stopped her quickly with, "Don't worry. When you get some work, then you can take care of it."

With a truly thankful smile, she leaned across the desk, kissed him lightly on the cheek, and whispered, "Thanks, Frank. Good night."

Leaving a blushing Frank behind, instead of heading for the elevator, strangely, she walked through the front door and back out into the dark night. She had barely walked a block when lightning flickered in the distance. And then the dull roar of thunder came–it too, still far off in the distance. *Brother*, she thought. *Wish I could afford a cab.*

Suddenly, she had something else to think about other then the approaching storm. She knew the sounds of someone following her. She had been followed before and learned how the footsteps followed hers, exactly in the same cadence, so you couldn't really tell if anyone was actually back there or not–until you stopped quickly and unexpectedly–and heard that one, telltale foot fall, just when it shouldn't have. So she stopped quickly, and sure enough, that errant foot did fall behind her. She was scared. Really scared, because the other time it had happened, luckily, a cop had been nearby and had quickly grabbed the man–an out-of-town, drunk conventioneer, looking for a good time–and taken him to jail to sober up.

But tonight, there was no one to help and the weather was turning bad. She had walked just far enough so that there were no lighted entryways to step into. In this part of New York, mostly day shops and the like–everything was already closed. The all-night clubs and restaurants were behind her–back the other way toward The Plaza–so she had to think. She walked faster now, and so did the footsteps behind her. *Were they getting closer?* she feared. She took one quick and cautious look around, but saw nothing. No one.

Then she scurried across the next street and up on the curb, just as a the first bolt of lightning zaaapped–right over her head–or at least it seemed that way. Now came the rain. First, just an occasional, huge drop went splat on the sidewalk. Then another and another cascaded down in the streetlights, turning the pavement in front of her into what looked like a polka dotted ribbon which ran ahead of her toward the next streetlight. The sidewalk turned suddenly as dark as the night as the drops came hurtling down–pelting her–stinging her head with no hat on it. It was a deluge.

It was raining too hard to hear the footsteps behind her now. In fact, she couldn't even hear her own. She knew she was in trouble, as she walked faster and faster.

Quickly she turned a corner and ducked into an alleyway. Maybe he wouldn't see that she had. Beneath an outside stairwell she had some protection from the storm. She crouched down, out of sight–she hoped. Out of the rain, she could finally hear again, and her heart almost stopped as she heard the footsteps–coming closer now–as they stopped, paused for a few breathtaking moments, then also turned slowly and relentlessly into the alley.

Alice crouched lower and lower in her hiding place, as the footsteps, ever so slowly, approached the exact place where she hid. Suddenly, a few inches from her hiding place, they stopped. Her eyes were wide open and filled with horror as she realized she had been found. Terror stricken, she held her breath and prepared to defend herself.

She raised the only weapon she had, her purse, high above her head, and as she did, a sudden flash of lightning illuminated a face. It was Ti, who smiled, looked down at her and said innocently, "Damn, Alice. Did I scare you?"

Barely able to breathe, Alice lowered her purse and said, "Me? Scared?" Her hands were shaking the purse above her, so she lowered it, as she rose to her feet and continued, "Absolutely not. No. Not at all."

A wet cat jumped off a trash can causing the lid to clang as it hit the pavement. Alice screamed and fell into Ti's arms. Recovering, she reluctantly admitted to a smiling Ti, "Well, maybe just a little."

"Sorry about that, Alice, but you shouldn't be out this late by yourself."

"Well, what are you doing out here?"

"Just waiting to see you home, Alice. All the way home."

It was raining hard as Ti and Alice, soaked to the bone, arrived in front of a shabby-looking apartment building. Alice noticed as Ti took a hard look at the decrepit place.

A little embarrassed, she admitted, "Well, this is it. Really."

They ran up the front steps, opened the front door and went quickly inside, finally out of the driving rain.

As Ti looked around the run-down place, she said, "Look—about The Plaza. How did you know?"

He continued to look around the drab surroundings as if taking inventory, "Not too hard to figure. The odds on a girl who's not working regular, living in a place like that are long, Alice, real long. 'Less she's a call girl."

Her eyes flashed as she looked him straight in his. "If that's what you think then—"

Ti calmly looked at her with admiration. "I don't think anything of the kind," he said. "I just think you get the real world and that make-believe world of the movies all mixed up."

"Well, let me explain something to you, Mister," she said with some anger. He had wounded her. "I have a much better chance of getting a big part in a movie if a producer thinks I don't need it. Know what I mean?" she said as she poked him in the chest for emphasis.

"Sure do." He took another admiring look at her. "Shows you were thinking, Alice. And that's something I value."

She smiled and turned—saying over her shoulder, "Come on. This way." Then she led him up three flights of stairs, into a dark hallway, past empty milk bottles and sacks of foul-smelling trash. At the end of the hallway, as she fumbled in her purse to find the key, a not-too-prosperous looking man in a dirty undershirt spoke loudly and angrily into a pay phone. "Hey. I said, hey! Yeah, you! You sonofabitch. Whada you mean, you're not gonna do it! Ya told me you were gonna do it! If you don't do it tomorrow, I'll be out ten bucks!"

Finding her key and seeing her neighbor's act was not playing well to Ti, Alice quickly opened the door and prepared to bid Ti to enter, when in the dim light, Alice saw an unwelcomed sight. It was a large woman, sitting in a chair at the end of the dark hallway, arms folded, as if she has been waiting for someone. And she had—Alice—who she greeted with a scowl on her face.

Alice glanced quickly at Ti as a warning, then smiled at the woman and said, too sweetly, "Why, Mrs. Bower."

Mrs. Bower was not impressed with her friendliness. She had more pressing concerns than civility. "And, hello to you, Miss—where have you been and why haven't you paid me—Reed. There's a matter of three months' past-due rent we need to talk about."

Alice was beyond embarrassed. This was a disaster. She had to buy some time, and tried with, "Can't we talk about it later?"

Standing up disgustedly, Mrs. Bower walked toward Alice, shaking her head from side to side. "This is later. I should have known better than to take an actress like you into a nice place like this." A roach picked that moment to run down the inner fat of her arm, and she flicked it off nonchalantly, as if she had had a lot of practice.

Alice, mortified, looked at Ti and in non-stop, guilt-driven thoughts, she pleaded to herself, *Oh God! Just take me now. Finally–finally I meet a decent guy–well, maybe he does carry a gun–but he seems okay, and here's old Mrs. Bower, ruining it all–acting like I'm a deadbeat, well, maybe I am a bit late with the money, but...*

Her thoughts were interrupted as Mrs. Bower–who was momentarily distracted as she hurried after the cockroach, caught it, then stepped on it with a splaat–started her harangue again.

"Truth is–you show biz people are all alike. Like peas in a pod. Take that vaudeville goof ball with the monkey–skipped out owing me four months rent." She shook her head at her own stupidity. "No ma'am, if you can't pay the sixty dollars right now..."

Alice's heart sunk. *It's over*, she thought. But,

a mischievous Ti winked at her secretly, then turned to the ranting landlady and said, "Excuse me for interrupting, Mrs. Bower." He held his hand up as if it were a monumental moment as he turned to a wet, shivering Alice and said, as if shocked, "Do you mean your new contract hasn't gotten here yet? Am I embarrassed!"

Alice looked like she had been kicked in the face by a mule. *What*? she thought.

Ti continued, "Now, Miss Reed. Please, please don't hold this against me or the studio."

Mrs. Bower's lips silently formed the word studio just as happily as if she were saying money. Ti continued, "Somebody as important as you shouldn't have to concern yourself with money! Heads will roll back at my office, I can assure you of that!"

Mrs. Bower was all smiles as she leaned into Ti's face and said, "Contract? Money?"

If there was any doubt in Mrs. Bower's monetary mind, it evaporated the instant Ti reached into his pocket and took out a super-sized roll of one hundred dollar bills.

With Mrs. Bower's eyes bulging, he continued, "Miss Reed, would you please accept as little as three hundred dollars on account?" He quickly handed Alice three crisp, one-hundred dollar bills. "I assure you, just as soon as we can wire the main office tomorrow morning, we can–"

Sensing a breakthrough, Alice immediately

got into the act with, "An artist doesn't dirty her hands with money. That is not the reward. It is the enjoyment I bring those wonderful, wonderful people out there who..."

Ti looked quickly at Alice. *Enough*, he thought. He put his arm around Mrs. Bower and started walking her down the hall, casually handing her a crisp, new hundred dollar bill.

"Just so you'll remember to take real good care of Miss Reed."

"She's really gonna be a big star, huh?"

Ti and Mrs. Bower both turned and looked at Alice as if they were studying Mary Pickford.

Ti cocked his head as if he were an artist, or director, trying to absorb the rare vision in front of his eyes. "Just look at her. Can't you tell?"

Mrs. Bower also looked at her tenant closely, in a totally new way. The rain had made Alice's mascara run down from her eyes, down across her face, almost to her jaw line. Halloween makeup couldn't have been better applied. She looked just like a fright doll.

But, Mrs. Bower could only see the dollar signs. "My, yes. She does have a certain look, now that you come to mention it."

Ti moved Mrs. Bower along saying, "Good night, now. She needs her beauty sleep."

Deep in thought, Mrs. Bower turned back toward Alice and over her shoulder in a new, deeply affectionate tone, she said, "Good night, my dear."

As Mrs. Bower descended the stairs, Alice could not resist milking it. She walked to the railing overlooking the stairs, and said demurely, "Mrs. Bower!"

Hearing her name, Mrs. Bower stopped and then looked up at Alice peering over the railing. Alice was never more dramatic in her life than when she said, "No matter how high my star may rise, surely you must know I'll never forget all of you little people who have helped me along the way."

Mrs. Bower bought the whole program, smiled, and continued down the stairs, deep in thought. Alice tried hard and succeeded in not laughing as she quickly opened her door and pulled a delighted Ti inside saying, "I'll be back in a second." She dashed into the bathroom to dry off, leaving Ti to look around the cluttered room.

He occupied himself by reading the sayings Alice had industriously tacked up on her walls. He studied each one and thought each title through.

Faith can move mountains. Winners never quit. Ask, and it shall be given you.

When Alice returned a few moments later with a clean face, and a towel around her neck which she was using to dry her hair, she saw Ti reading her self-help thoughts.

She was glad he was doing that. Maybe they shared some thought up there on the wall. She said, "See anything you like?"

"As a matter of fact, I do." he said. And, he did like what he saw, very much. But it wasn't hanging on the wall. It was standing right in front of him, and he looked it over carefully from the red shoes, right up to the top of her wet head. And that didn't bother Alice. Not one bit. In fact, she liked it. She liked the way he looked at her. She smiled–even blushed a little–as she moved closer to him and put the three hundred dollars in his lapel pocket.

"Thanks for the loan. I normally don't do that." She added firmly, "And I mean that."

"And I believe that," he said as he tried to give the money back to her.

She blocked his hand with hers, and said, "No. I won't take it. I can't."

He knew there was more to that than the words she had said. And he noticed that there was a relaxed, thankful, almost happy sound to her voice for the first time since the rain had started. He liked to hear her that way.

As he took both ends of the towel which still hung loosely around her beautiful neck, and gently pulled her closer to him, she said, "Thanks to you, she won't be bothering me anymore."

"But I might," he said quietly. She smiled her approval, and they kissed for a long moment.

Now, there was another woman in Alvin Thomas's life.

Chapter 11

A Hot Time In The Old Town.

As Alice sat at a table in Lindy's with Ti, George and George's date, a blonde named, Cindy–she thought about the past week.

She could still smell the hot dogs with the spicy hot mustard and sauerkraut she had tasted for the very first time at Coney Island.

She could still hear the sound of the announcer saying, *"And they're off,"* at the race track–and the gifted voices of Fanny Brice and Will Rogers singing and joking at the Ziegfeld Follies.

It's been a great week, she thought. And she even remembered fondly, sitting patiently, watching Ti play an all-night game of poker with George and others. And then, unbelievably–even after that all-night game–contentedly sitting and watching him hit golf ball after golf ball–hour after hour in the early morning light at a practice range. *I even enjoyed watching him do that,* she thought, thinking back.

Certainly, she had been aware that he had played golf very well that day with Jack St. James, but it never occurred to her that there might have been a special reason why he had been able to make the putt when he had to–a reason other than he quite obviously had a lot of talent. But after all–others did, too.

So, it had to have been something else. Something more. And, when she saw the total concentration, the total dedication he gave to his practice, she finally understood *exactly* what it was.

She understood that somehow, someway–he had been able to develop an *incredible* desire to work at something–a desire that was so strong–that he was able to not only work at something until he had it right–but until he had it absolutely *perfect*. Maybe it sprang from something she did not yet understand. Maybe something in his childhood.

Maybe something else.

But, she did know that those questions about him–and others–attracted her to him. As did the mystery of although he thought it wrong to either drink or smoke–he had little problem with killing four men. True, they all had tried to either rob him–or kill him or someone close to him. But still, he was able to do that. And that added up to danger, which always has–and always will appeal to certain women–especially one like Alice.

So, as Alice sat in Lindy's watching Ti sip his cup of coffee, and George and Cindy dance, she felt very good. Very good indeed.

But the same could not be said for Jack St. James, who at that very moment, was trying his best not to pick up the telephone to call her. But– he failed, picked it up–then *slammed* it down–as he looked mournfully up at a calendar above the phone and regretfully saw that only five days had been marked off.

———————

The next morning, George sat at a table in a coffee shop, reading a headline in *The New York Times* which proclaimed:

CITY'S COLDEST WINTER
IN 40 YEARS PREDICTED

George tried not to pay attention to an agitated Ti who sat across the table and tugged at his coat sleeve, saying anxiously, "George. George!"

"Uh... yeah, Ti?"

"I said–any word from my favorite millionaire?"

George concealed a pained look on his face as he answered, "Ti–give me a break. Please. Let's don't do Howard Fucking Hughes today. Okay?"

"George, we'll do Howard Fucking Hughes

until you get me that game you promised."

"I said I'd try. Hell, I *am* trying. I'm always trying. You know that! But it's like chasing fog. The only thing I know is what everybody else knows. He flies airplanes, makes movies and loves golf and beautiful women. Other than that I don't know shit."

In a moment of self pity, George said, "Why do I get jobs like this?"

"For twenty percent of my action."

"But there are a lot of rich guys. Why him? Why Hughes?"

George knew full well why, but he also knew this would get Ti started and give him a chance to maybe vent his spleen. As George buried his head behind *The New York Times*, he let nature take its course.

"I'll tell you why, George," Ti started off, so intent his voice quivered. "Because Howard Hughes had a daddy who died early and left him the patent on a diamond drilling bit. So, nearly every oil man in the country pays Howard Hughes a royalty, which means that every morning, just by opening his mail, Hughes makes more money than we see in a whole year. And *that* makes Howard Hughes, George, the richest man in this country. And there's another reason George–an even better reason, George. Howard Hughes loves to play golf–and is good enough to think he may be able to beat me."

George didn't answer. He just continued to hide behind *The New York Times*, confident that this plan was working. He figured that Ti would expend all of his considerable energy on this early morning's Hughes tirade, leaving him the rest of the day in peace–at least as far as the Hughes topic was concerned.

"So, George. Just do your part and get me a golf match with Hughes. I'll win a million dollars from him. Then *I'll* be a millionaire, too–and I won't have to worry about making money anymore. In fact, I'll be so rich, they'll ask me to join one of those high brow country clubs."

"Okay. Okay! But it won't be easy. Hughes won't play with anybody unless they are somebody."

"*Are*, somebody? I–*are*–somebody! Why not me?"

"Because he's rich and while you are certainly not hurting–money wise–you are not *big* rich. You are *not* in his league. Not even close! I repeat–he is rich–and you are *not*! So, Ti! If he doesn't want to play golf with you for a million dollars–he won't! He doesn't *have* to!"

"He makes the rules, huh?" Ti said with total absorption. He thought for a minute, then continued, "Okay. Okay. When I was standing back on the fourteenth tee at Long Island Country Club last week–I was thinking–I was thinking–Alvin Thomas, *you* can hit a golf ball five hundred yards from this tee." He looked far off in the distance as if reconsidering.

"Yep. I know I can. I know I can do it!"

Then seeming to have finally made up his mind, he said, "So, George. Would Howard Hughes play me then? Would I be *somebody* if I could do that?"

George was puzzled, but said, "You mean if you actually hit a golf ball five hundred yards, from the fourteenth tee at the Long Island Country Club?"

"Yeah. Would he play me then?"

"Uh–well, sure–yeah–uh, maybe. *Maybe* he would. Oh hell, how do I know?" he said as he looked strangely at Ti. "Look. Are you *really* talking about hitting a golf ball off the fourteenth tee at The Long Island Country Club and hitting it five-hundred yards? Or, are you talking about hustling Jack St. James with some trick and actually teeing the ball up on Broadway or some other man-made street? That would be easy. He won't go for that!"

"Right, George. Right! I agree. And anybody who would hit a golf ball down a road to win a bet and try to screw somebody out of a few bucks is nothing more than a no-class chickenshit."

"Can you do it? Can you really hit a golf ball five hundred yards off that fourteenth tee?"

"Well, not tomorrow for sure. It would take time to get ready. Maybe as much as six months.

Maybe more." Ti waited for the reality of the thought to sink in, then he continued. "But if St. James wants–he has a month to accept the bet I offered."

"Bet! You offered him a bet!! How much?"

"Whatever he wants."

George was stunned. "Yeah? Well, Ti. Look– I'm not doubting you–but how are you going to do it?"

Ti smiled softly and said, "George. If I tell you, I'll lose the power."

"What power?"

"The power of being the only one who knows."

"Fine! Don't tell me."

Ti just smiled and watched George crumple up his *New York Times*, toss a couple of dollars on the table, and leave, steaming.

If I plan this right, this might all be worth it, Ti thought.

———————

At Lindy's restaurant the next night, a doorman was busy, as he greeted couple after couple who streamed into the place looking for fun. These were the beautiful people and tonight, the beautiful people seemed especially ready for fun.

One table in particular was feeling no pain.

Seated on one side of it was George and his bored date, Laverne. Across from them sat Margo, a curvaceous blonde showgirl, who not only had her plate full, but also the table top, where her date, out-of-town banker and notorious wild man, John Van Hauffwigin, was dancing, totally out of control.

Van Hauffwigin tried to dance something which looked like a cross between the Charleston and the black bottom as he screamed–for no apparent reason other than he could remember the words–*"Nuuu York! Nuuu York! Nuuu York! Nuuu York! Nuuu York! Nuuu York! Nuuu..."*

Even the loudest at other tables were amazed at Van Hauffwigin's craziness, which prompted even the patient Margo to scream, *"Okay, Hauffy. Right!* You're in New York. Not stuck at home in Beverly Hills. Okay? Hauffy! Can you hear me?"

But he couldn't. He was on fire with rhythm– but more with gin. Freed from all pretense of civility–and far from his palatial Los Angeles home–Van Hauffwigin simply continued to dance and shout, *"Nuuu York! Nuuu York! Nuuu York! Nuuu–"* with a silly smile plastered on his face.

George, bored, shook his head and grimaced as Laverne tugged at his sleeve, pointed across the room, and said, "Say–is that your friend, Ti, over there in the corner? He too good for us or something?"

"Naww. Just trying to make time with that

little sweetheart, Alice Reed. You know how it is. They want to be alone for awhile."

Ti saw George and Laverne looking—so George gave Ti a big wave and motioned for him to come on over.

Across the room, Ti just acknowledged the wave, looked back at Alice, and said, "Looks like everybody's watching us tonight."

"I spend a lot of my time watching people," she said.

"Yeah—I know what you mean. I have to watch people real careful in my business, too."

Alice laughed, "I'll bet you do. But I mean, watching people—the way they walk and talk—that's how you learn to act. You learn a lot about people that way."

"I'll bet you do."

"I've got a feeling that sometimes you have to do a little acting, too."

"Well, maybe I do, Alice. Maybe I do," Ti said. Suddenly he had a pained look on his face. "Oh no."

"What's the matter?"

Ti shielded his face with his hand, and said, "Damn. Notso just saw me."

"Notso?"

"Notso Fuqua. Can't seem to shake that guy."

Notso smiled and walked toward their table, and as he did, Alice couldn't help but study him. He was short, fat, loudly dressed, used tons of greasy pomade on his hair, and in general, looked like the very definition of stupid. She immediately felt a little sorry for him.

Notso reached the table, and with hat in hand, he nodded respectfully to Alice saying, "How you, ma'am?" Then he looked pleadingly at Ti and said, "Ti, have ya thought anymore about us workin' a proposition together?"

Ti was like ice as he answered, "Nothin' to think about, Notso. Just not interested."

Notso was distraught. "Aw, Ti! I'd do anything. Anything! I mean, you name it. I'd do it, and I'd do it gladly. Just some little somethin'?"

"Notso, the lady and I are trying to have some dinner. I'll thank you to let us get back to it."

"But Ti, I gotta get something goin'. It's been so long since I made anything, well–"

Ti reached into his pocket, pulled out a fifty dollar bill and handed it to him. "Sure. I understand," he said quietly. "Maybe this will help."

Notso quickly took the bill and stuffed it in his pocket. "Thanks, Ti." He smiled and nodded to Alice. "Good night."

Alice watched Notso walk away, and said, "I think I know the answer to this, but why do they call him Notso?"

"Because he's not-so-smart. But worse than that Alice..." Ti paused for dramatic effect. "He's a killer."

Alice's head jerked in Notso's direction. "What? My God! And I thought I knew people. In a million years, Ti–in a million years! I never would have guessed that."

She turned and took one more look at the departing Notso. "A killer–and you're sure?"

"Absolutely. He's not real smart. And he tells everything he knows. He can kill you, all right."

Alice smiled her understanding. In Ti's business, she was learning, information was everything.

"You really do have to keep your guard up, don't you?"

"All the time. I've got a reputation and everybody wants to trade off of it, one way or another."

"How?"

"Well, they either want to work a proposition with me and take all the credit for it later, or–they want to square off against me and be the one who outwitted old Ti."

She toasted him with her glass of champagne and said, "Here's hoping you're never outwitted."

He returned the toast with his cup of coffee, and said, "I'll drink to that."

George walked up and said excitedly, "Ti, Flynn wants to talk a little business with us."

"I'll stay here," Alice said, sensing this might be confidential. Ti nodded and he and George walked over to Leo Flynn's table and sat down.

George knew the pecking order in this deal and decided to keep his mouth shut and just listen, which was more than Van Hauffwigin–still screaming at the top of his lungs and dancing across the room–could do.

Ti listened seriously as Flynn said, "Your first match will be in two weeks. You'll play the club champion over at..."

Flynn was suddenly drowned out by Van Hauffwigin's voice–a scant few feet away. He had joined a conga line, and was shaking his hips, while doing his best to help Margo do the same in front of him–as he screamed, *"Nuuu York! Nuuu York! Nuuu York! Nuuu York! Nuuu York! Nuuu York!"*

Flynn waited a minute until the line had moved on, then said with a frown, "Damn. Somebody ought to either shut that idiot up–or teach him the name of another town!"

George shook his head and quickly said, "He's a rich banker from the west coast." Embarrassed, he added meekly, "Business associate of mine."

Flynn turned his attention back to Ti and the deal. "Anyway–your first match will be at Grassy Sprain Country Club against their club champion–Don McLean. He just won some kind of piddly-squat amateur championship somewhere in Virginia–maybe it was Pequoia."

Flynn shook his head at the absurdity of what he was about to say. "He wins a silly, shiny trophy in some tournament in Nowhere, U.S.A. Now everyone says he's good enough to play anybody. Truth is–it's those blue bloods at his club that are pushing him." He laughed at the idea. "One lousy trophy and they figure he's God's gift to golf–and nobody can beat him?"

He looked at Ti and delivered the kicker he knew Ti wanted to hear. "They're ready to match my money."

"How much?" Ti asked quickly.

"I told them I'd put up twenty big ones on you against McLean. Straight up. Match play."

"You that sure I can beat him?"

"He's too full of himself to have any respect for you. He's a country club boy. You–you're just a country boy. He thinks you're trash that backed up from the sewer."

He waited to see if that bothered Ti. It didn't, so he continued, "I mean, you ain't one of his kind–that's for sure." Then he remembered that it was time to dangle the first carrot. "Oh yeah–I picked up a nice fifty grand side bet."

"Fifty? I'll take half of that," Ti said quickly.

"Look. I match all the stakes. You get your share. My side bets are mine. Point is–this match will give you a chance to prove you're more than just a hustler. It's your chance to prove you really can play the game."

"Who says I want to?"

Flynn raised an eyebrow and said sternly,

"Anybody with real talent wants to prove that. Win–and this will put you in a whole new arena."

He leaned in a little closer to Ti, looked around to make sure no one was listening who shouldn't have been, and said quietly, "But here's the big carrot. If you can survive playing the best players from the East coast clubs, you have a chance–now listen good–I said a chance, to be invited to the big-money tournament on the west coast this winter."

"Why just a chance?"

Flynn grinned. "Well–it's almost a social affair. You know, long tails and the like–and last time I looked, I didn't spot your name in the Astor's social register." He smiled at the thought of Ti dressed like a penguin. Then he got serious. "Look–this is about something you don't know anything about yet. It's about rich guys playing other rich guys for shiny trophies."

For the first time, Ti showed real anger to Leo. "Leo! Are you crazy? I'm not playing golf for some shiny damn trophy."

Flynn liked that outburst. It confirmed what he knew had to be true–even though he had never before seen it. He had finally met the real Ti, the fiery competitor who lay hidden beneath that cool veneer. *Well, hello Mister Ti*, he thought. *Nice to finally meet you–and welcome to the game.* But aloud he said, "Hold on, Ti. The night before the tournament there's a big whing ding called a

144

Calcutta."

"A what?"

"Don't worry about it. Remember Calcutta, okay? Anyway, everybody bids on a player and all the money goes in a pool. The guy who buys the winner get the whole pool of money. And Ti, we're talking about a deep fucking pool."

"Side bets accepted?"

Flynn smiled, "Well now–I wouldn't be at all surprised."

"Where are they playing?" Ti said eagerly.

"In Los Angeles at some spiffy place called El Rancho Country Club."

Flynn watched Ti for a long moment. He looked as though he was daydreaming. But he wasn't. No, he was focusing on two things. Flynn could almost see the wheels moving. The focus tightening. And he could almost hear Ti thinking–repeating over and over–*Calcutta. El Rancho Country Club.*

———————

That night, Ti and Alice were walking down the street in silence. Ti was busy thinking about his upcoming match with Virginia Champion, Don McLean, and Alice was looking at him quizzically, studying him, as she said, "You never did tell me how you got the name Titanic."

"Nothing special. Back when I was still on

the road, a guy named Snow Clark down in Joplin, Missouri, bet me I couldn't jump head first over a pool table without touching it. Well, I did, and won fifty dollars–a lot of money to me that day. Anyway–he just up and said, 'What is your name, boy?' After I told him, he said, 'Alvin Thomas, huh? Well, they oughta call you *Titanic*, 'cause you sink everybody who bets against you!' That's all there was to it."

"Interesting." She waited, and debated whether to broach the next subject, but she decided to go ahead and get to the truth. "So you weren't on the Titanic steam ship that went down...and you didn't dress up in women's clothes to get a seat on a lifeboat...and you didn't...?"

Ti laughed. "You already heard that one, huh?"

"Who would say something like that?"

"Simpletons, Alice. Guys like Notso who make up stories they think other morons will believe–to make them feel like a big man."

"To make a trap for fools..." she said, knowingly.

"Huh?" Ti said.

"Oh nothing, just something Kipling wrote." Now, she liked him even more. *He must really be something special*, she thought. *Otherwise they wouldn't go to so much trouble trying to tear him down and discredit him.*

"Alice, the truth is, as far as you're concerned,

my life's pretty much an open book. You can ask me damned near anything you want–within reason."

She never dreamed she'd get an invitation like that–so she quickly grabbed it. "Okay, then. So, what made you decide to be a gambler?"

"Everybody's a gambler, Alice. Farmers back in Arkansas gamble on rain. They call that faith. Millions of people in this country gamble on the stock market. That's an investment. Actors like you, gamble they'll get another part. That's believing in yourself. I'm just a little more obvious than the rest."

"You mean honest?"

"That depends on how you define honest." *Maybe she's not quite ready to hear my peanut story*, he thought.

"I'm a gambler. Pure and simple. I use cards, dice, coins or anything else I can think of to win a bet or make a proposition work."

"Hmmm. All right. Let's talk about the kind of gambling you do. How in the world did you learn? Is there a book on that?"

"No, Alice, but if there were, I'd know most of it by heart."

"Tell me about it."

"It would be a long book––but if you want–I can give you a couple of pages off the top of my head."

"Shoot."

"Okay–first, let's talk about cards."

Playing along, Alice nodded. "Cards, right!"

She noticed how serious he suddenly became as he closed his eyes and recited from memory. "The chances of holding a pair in a five-card hand are nearly dead even–one hundred and three to one hundred–to be exact. The odds are in your favor if you bet on holding a spade higher than an eight on a five card draw. You see, it will generally take eight and one-half cards to get the first ace."

If he only knew, I have absolutely no earthly idea! she thought.

"Now dice. To throw an ace, twice, it's nine and eight tenths rolls. It takes twenty-four and one-half rolls to throw a total of twelve–with two sixes on the dice. With twenty-four and one-half rolls, the odds are dead even. To throw two sixes–twice–it's different. A lot different."

Totally lost, she decided to bull the game, and added eagerly, "I should certainly imagine it would be a lot different."

"Right. It takes sixty rolls to throw two sixes–twice on the pair of dice. Most people would assume that if you can throw those two sixes once in twenty four rolls–then logically you'd throw those four sixes in forty eight rolls. Right?"

Alice was lost. Just guessing, she decided to agree with him. "Uh, that seems more than logical to me?"

"Wrong! The odds are, it will take sixty rolls

to do that."

"Just testing you, Ti!"

"But see? You have to keep these odds in your mind all the time when you're gambling. So, even if an opponent may be cheating you, so that he may win the pot, you can absolutely clean him out on side bets. I know it sounds strange, but in that situation, you can afford to lose the war, because you'll be winning all the little battles–the side bets– and that makes you the man in control. Got it?"

"Look at me. Don't I look like I got it?"

"Now take flipping coins..."

Ti let's don't take flipping coins, she thought. *Let's just forget I ever asked about...*

"If you call the three coins, it's five to three. If you call four coins–it's five to three. If you call the three coins, you call two tails and a head, which remember, is five to three."

"Right!" *Who could forget those memorable words–five to three?* she thought.

"Now, if you call four coins, you call two heads and two tails, which again is five to three. Most people would think the odds would be five or six to one..."

Alice just shook her head in agreement. He wouldn't wait for her to answer, anyway. He was on a roll. *A boring roll,* she thought. But a roll, nonetheless. She tried to keep the semblance of a smile on her lips, but it wasn't easy.

"... Not true. And this is where it gets really

interesting. If they call two to one, you've still got the edge, because instead of laying a five to three bet you'd..." He stopped abruptly as he noticed that Alice's eyes were starting to wall.

"Damn. I think I'm boring you, Alice. That's the same look George gets when I try to explain this stuff to him."

"Ti. I am truly amazed. But I don't have an inkling of what you're talking about."

"Well, sure you do, Alice. You're a smart woman and..."

"I'm not that kind of smart, Ti. Most people aren't. You're like a...a...an engineer! That's it. It's like you have to break everything down to the smallest detail, then you have to draw up some kind of master plan to construct something."

"You put it that way, Alice. Maybe you're right. Some day remind me to tell you about the way I reconstructed a peanut."

He changed the subject. "The point is, I learned early on I couldn't depend on my luck. So, I figured for me to be a winner, I'd need something I could depend on. Some kind of skillful advantage. You know—something to give me a little edge."

"Makes sense to me." *Good, he's talking English again,* she thought.

"That's where a friend of mine came in. Taught me about the laws of probability. Some people call them the odds. He taught me to use them correctly with cards, dice and coins."

"So, by using these odds, there's a strong probability you are going to win?" she asked.

"Probability? Alice, it's a certainty. If you know what to look for when you're gambling. Numbers, combinations, percentages. Each one will fall into place like a lynchpin and at just the right time–if you understand the unfailing law of mathematical probability–the odds. Alice, when it's all said and done, the odds teach you one thing and one thing only. There's just no such thing as luck."

Mesmerized, she looked at him in amazement. *Wow! If I had a mind and a memory like that, I would have no problem learning my lines,* she thought. Then she said, "The man who taught you–the man who could write the book–he sounds almost super human."

Then, in a playful, mysterious way, he stopped, pulled her to him and looking deep into her eyes said, "He is, Alice. Now, how'd you like to meet a wizard?"

Chapter 12

Off To See
The Wizard...

Professor Malloy, an older man, was dressed in trousers, white shirt, bow tie and suspenders–and a pair of well-worn spectacles perched delicately on the end of his nose.

Ti and Alice were already sipping their drinks as they sat across from him in his cluttered but interesting study. While they waited respectfully for him to take his glass of wine from his housekeeper's tray, they studied a very large, glass-encased artist's drawing of a sinking ship–prominently displayed on the Professor's wall.

An accompanying newspaper headline read:

H.M.S. TITANIC SINKS!
OVER 1500 SOULS LOST!

When the Professor turned back to them, he took a sip of wine and then met their gaze.

Ti said, "Without Professor Malloy here, I wouldn't be where I am today. He gave me a skillful advantage. Taught me the odds on everything from cards to dice." He looked at the Professor with genuine respect and Alice, watching, felt that there was a special place in Ti's heart for this interesting man.

Ti continued, "That's why I call him the wizard of the Bronx."

One look at the Professor's face and Alice could tell he liked his nickname. And liked it well. It was not beauty, but brains that the Professor valued most, even though one look at Alice had made him ready to make an exception in her case.

Still, his face fairly glowed as he accepted the compliment. "It's true. I did teach Mister Ti all about my hobby–knowing the odds–like exactly when the next ace will fall, or when you will or will not match up a certain card," said the Professor. "But, the truth is, I had good reason to make the effort–to spend time, which at my age, I have precious little of. My reasoning was actually very simple. I simply had not met–in all my years of academia–anyone who possessed such incredible brainpower, as well as the desire to succeed. So, when I met him, not only did I appreciate his unique nickname–Titanic–I quickly recognized his potential. I flatter myself to think that I instinctively knew that with his kind of gifts, Mister Ti could become the biggest thing to ever hit New York's gambling community–if–and only if–he also had the common sense to understand one thing."

"Which was?" Alice eagerly asked.

"Simply this. No matter how certain it may appear–no matter how absolutely sure you are–if anything can go wrong–it will. It is knowing that fact of nature–and planning for it–which will get one past those rainy days, which will come. However, although knowing the odds and applying them correctly is a huge advantage–still–there are no sure things. No guarantees. You simply can not tempt fate."

He nodded at the big picture of the ship, *Titanic*, sinking. "They believed she was impregnable. And why not? The *Titanic* was world-class–as were its builders. But something could go wrong–and it did. Terribly. This tragedy teaches us that if you flaunt your supposed wisdom in the face of destiny–she will seek her revenge. And, the results can be tragic."

The old man looked longingly at the doomed ship on the wall. Then, he turned and raised his glass of wine to the young couple across the small room from him. "But enough. Mister Ti. Here's to you and your young lady."

Alice and the Professor toasted each other and took sips of wine, as Ti drank his coffee.

The Professor looked fondly at Ti.

"Now, how's your golf?" He looked at Alice

and said, "Young lady. I've tried to explain to him that with the proper combination of mathematical knowledge–his innate athletic skills, and that most illusive, most intangible ingredient of all–"

Alice knew this answer, too, "Maybe a little acting, Professor. A little drama?"

The Professor was both delighted and surprised that she would know so much about it. "Well, yes! Yes, indeed. A little drama is good for any game–might even be an element he could use to, shall we say, confuse the issue–so to speak. And, well, who knows? Although I do not know for sure, it is possible that golf might very well prove to be almost as profitable for him as cards."

Ti smiled and said respectfully, "As a matter of fact, I've been working on that, Professor."

They all smiled. Ti looked at his watch and added, "We'd better be going."

Knowing Ti might like a private moment to say a personal word to the Professor, Alice headed toward the hall, saying, "I'll get my coat. Please don't get up."

The Professor watched her leave, then said, "I like that girl, Mister Ti. Independent. Good attitude. She could be a real help to you."

Ti liked that. But instead of agreeing, feigned defensiveness and said, "Hey! You trying to get me married off?"

With a wink, the Professor said, "It never hurts a man to have a good partner. Who knows?

She may even bring you luck."

Ti looked genuinely puzzled as he said seriously, "Luck? I thought you and I agreed there is no such thing as luck."

"Well some people spend a wonderful life in ignorant bliss. And for somebody as–shall we say– as intense as you, that might be an extraordinary complement," the Professor said with a knowing look.

It was not lost on Ti.

Chapter 13

Enter
"The Fox"

At a private airport outside the growing town of Los Angeles, California, a single-engine airplane dropped swiftly from a cloudless sky, leveled out and touched down on the runway where it bounced once–twice–then came quickly to a stop in front of a black Cadillac.

A tall, dark-haired, solitary man, wearing an aviator's cap and a three-day growth of beard, stepped out of the cockpit and onto the wing. He reached into the back seat of the plane, pulled out one piece of luggage and a set of golf clubs, and casually dropped them both to the ground.

A chauffeur, Daryl, hurried toward the plane, wisely disregarded the luggage, quickly picked up the golf clubs and greeted the man with, "Good trip, Mr. Hughes?"

As always, Howard Hughes spoke in a high-pitched, whiny voice as he said, "Awww, it was all right, Daryl. Just didn't see one damn golf course the whole time." He then dropped lightly down to the ground and took a golf club and ball out of his golf bag which Daryl held for him. Hughes dropped the ball on the ground and addressed it with his club which he then effortlessly swung sending the ball rocketing out of sight.

Not kissing up to Hughes, just greatly impressed at the natural ability of his boss, Daryl smiled and said with awe, "Well struck."

"Yeah," Hughes agreed nonchalantly. "You know, Daryl. There's just nothing like the feel of a drive you hit right in the screws. But hell–you wouldn't know, would you?" He didn't even wait for an answer, "You know what my problem is? I got nobody to play with!"

Daryl started toward the car with the bags as Hughes walked alongside him carrying his golf bag. "Either they are scared to play me because they're not good enough–or they're scared to play me, because I've got so damn much money–that they know I'll just drown 'em."

Hughes stopped, looked Daryl in the eye and said in a low voice which sounded like a child's confession, "Ya know–I did that once, Daryl. I damn sure did. This sonofabitch had me down three strokes with only two holes to play. Two holes– hell he had me! So, I just up and said–I said, 'Hey! How about a brand new bet on these last two holes?' He said, 'Sure Howard. Fine with me.' So,

I said, 'Okay, sonofabitch, we're going to play these last two holes for a million damn dollars.' "

Hughes purposely waited in silence.

"And?" Daryl said.

"Poor sonofabitch started crying. Sat down on the ground and started crying like a baby–just like a little baby." Hughes started walking on toward the car. "Daryl. I should never have done that," he said quietly with sincere remorse.

Daryl was impressed. This was the very first time he could ever remember when his boss had actually expressed regret for his actions. Overwhelmed, he emphatically agreed, "No sir! You certainly should not have done that!"

Hughes nodded, "You're damn right I shouldn't have. Hell, that story got around–and I've had a pisser of a time getting an interesting game ever since."

Daryl shook his head. *I should have known,* he thought.

Hughes went on with his pitiful story. "That's the problem when a million dollars doesn't mean that much to you." He looked at Daryl as if this was an important warning. "Don't ever let that happen to you, Daryl."

"Don't worry," Daryl said almost imperceptibly under his breath.

They reached the car, both got in, and Daryl looked in the rear view mirror for his instructions. "Where to Mr. Hughes?"

"The movie studio. Then I'm going to hit some balls at the club."

―――――――――

In his ultra-luxurious New York City apartment, Jack St. James was approaching a state of apoplexy as he walked past his telephone for the fifty-third time–he was counting–stopped, picked up the receiver, then quickly slammed it down.

He looked up on the wall above the phone, and frantically studied a calendar which had only twenty days marked off.

Damn! he thought for the fifty-third time. Then he walked on, and repeated the whole process.

―――――――――

The next day dawned clear and bright for the first of the big East coast money matches. In the parking lot just outside the Grassy Sprain Golf Club, Ti's opponent for the day–the carefree Don McLean, known as The Fox, whistled a happy tune as he pulled his golf bag out of his trunk and prepared to close it.

"Oops!" McLean said as he accidentally dropped a ball and watched helplessly as it bounced quickly away, down the pavement. But when a hand came out of nowhere, deftly scooped up the ball and flipped it back to him, McLean smiled and thought, *Must be my lucky day!*

The man who had caught the ball was Ti and he walked toward McLean with a big, friendly smile.

Out on the course on the first tee, Alice, George, the Professor, Flynn and the reporter, Turner, all waited expectantly for McLean and Ti to arrive.

Nearby, at least a dozen Grassy Sprain members also waited to cheer McLean on. Among that group were two, out-of-town guests, none other than Ti's old adversaries from Cincinnati, Gus and Milburn.

One Grassy Sprain member had his arms around both Gus and Milburn, in a fraternal embrace, as he said, "Glad you boys could come in for the big match."

Gus answered quickly and emphatically, "Wouldn't have missed it for anything–thanks for the invite."

The member answered, "Our kind have to stick together."

Another member said, "The smartest thing we ever did was put our money on McLean. Smart golfer!"

Another said, "They don't call him 'The Fox' for nothing."

Gus and Milburn nodded and then drifted

away from the group, chain-smoking, barely able to control their self-appreciating glee. *Ah ha!* Milburn smugly thought. *Alvin Thomas–or Titanic–or whoever he is, will finally get his comeuppance today.*

Looking as if he had just made up his mind about something, Gus said, "Milburn, yes, I do want to buy the home in Florida next to yours." A thought struck him. "Wait! What if he pays us off with a check and not cash today! Can I simply sign it over to you–is that permissible?"

"Certainly, that will be fine, and I think that using your winnings in such a manner will create an excellent investment for the future. Every time we visit Florida and the new home, we'll think of what a wonderful way we made up for our earlier misfortune at the hands of...well, speak of the devil."

He smiled and pointed at Ti and McLean as they walked slowly toward the first tee.

The Fox was older than Ti. A no-nonsense, confident, highly intelligent man, who barely listened as Ti blurted out, "This is a real honor. Playing against Don McLean, The Fox! Not only the champion of this club–but also the champion of the Pequoia Invitational in–in...?"

"Pequoia, Virginia," McLean said, a little annoyed that Thomas didn't know about his latest victory.

Ti whistled softly, in awe, and said, "You

really must be something."

McLean didn't have time for this. He said, "I hear they call you Titanic? What kind of damn name is that?"

Ti laughed aloud. "A damn silly name, isn't it? Well my real name is Thomas. Just plain old Alvin Clarence Thomas out of Rogers, Arkansas."

"Play much golf back in Arkansas, Thomas?"

"Never. Not a lick. But I've been getting out and trying to play a lot the past few years here in New York–and I like it. I really do."

Ti looked closely at the supremely confident McLean. "With all your tournament experience, I'll bet you haven't got a nerve in your whole body."

Ti looked around to make sure no one was listening, and lowered his voice to deliver the mind numbing subject he had mastered so well. "Say. How much money have you won? Come on–you can tell me!"

The group on the first tee saw McLean and Ti had stopped, and were standing under a shade tree as an animated Ti gestured with his hands.

Alice was a little confused as she asked George, "I wonder why they don't come on up here and start the game?"

George smiled and said. "Alice. The game has already started." Turner nodded his agreement.

Ti walked away from McLean, whose eyes reflected a primal, gut-wrenching fear. The Fox caught up with the quick-striding Ti, who was now well into his act–the part where he was engrossed in his elaborately choreographed, deep-breathing exercises and muscle stretching.

To better understand what he was actually up against, McLean, trying to act casual, said, "So, you have played for money before, huh?"

Ti said nothing. He just walked on.

"Uh, say uhh–how come you didn't–uh–didn't play in the Pequoia Invitational tournament I just won?"

Ti never broke stride as he said coldly, "Hell. I don't care anything about trophies. Not a damn thing."

Then he pointed ahead and said brightly, "Hey! Are those two more of your friends up there? Is that old Gus and Milburn, all the way from Cincinnati? Well hell! You've got a whole damned army up there–all betting on you!"

"Uh, yeah, well–I guess I've got some supporters all right–but you didn't tell me why you didn't..."

Ti had no more time for answers. It was time to sink the harpoon, and he did it quickly and neatly with, "I bet they're saying there's just no way you can lose. Yep. The kind of serious money Grassy Sprain and now, Cincinnati, is betting on you, well it proves they sure have faith in you. Must be a great feeling."

As an afterthought, he quietly buried him

with, "Of course, I wouldn't want a big responsibility like that. No sir. I'm just not cut out for that kind of pressure. Not me."

McLean's hypnotically blank stare would have qualified as a highlight from a zombie ritual in Haiti, as he numbly arrived at the first tee box along with a smiling, relaxed Ti.

McLean stumbled over the tee marker. Then, as his caddy offered him his driver, he first fumbled, then dropped it, then bent over to pick it up–and as he did–his sunglasses fell out of his pocket–which he grabbed at–but also dropped, then stepped on, breaking them into a dozen pieces.

Gus and Milburn saw none of the impending disaster because they were blinded by their hatred for Ti. It was so strong that as Ti stopped by to say hello, it was all Milburn and Gus could do not to laugh in his face.

"We've waited a long time for this day," Gus said with total confidence. Noticing that Alice, George, the Professor and Flynn were looking on, to rub it in, Gus mockingly said to Ti, "I hear you want to make a personal bet. Got your money?"

"You bet. Twenty-five thousand dollars," Ti said evenly as he handed Gus a big roll of bills. Milburn quickly counted the money and marked a note pad. Then he said, as if he had just locked the door of Ti's prison cell, "That's it. You are covered."

The match on the verge of starting, to no one–

but to everyone–Ti said, "You know. This is gonna be fun. Even though everybody knows I don't have much of a chance."

Gus couldn't help but answer. "Damn, Thomas! What happened to all that confidence?" he said as he laughed and was joined by the Grassy Sprain members.

Milburn added loudly and with a know-it-all grin, "A chicken cackles real loud until The Fox from Pequoia has got him by the throat."

McLean stood on the tee box, next to Ti, and blankly watched a quick coin flip by a Grassy Sprain member. In the space of those few moments–and unseen by his supporters–the automatized McLean managed to pour a glass of drinking water down the front of his shirt–and fumble for his tee and somehow drop it down his pants into his crotch.

Ti had the honors and teed his ball up, stole a satisfied glance at McLean, and then rifled his ball far down the fairway, dead center.

McLean walked to the front of the tee box where he again tripped over the marker. He cursed the groundskeepers who had put it out there in his way–and then teed his ball up, after at least three attempts–because he had put the tee in at an awkward angle. Finally, to relax, he waggled his club a few times, but in so doing, he inadvertently let the driver slip from his sweaty hands, and somehow, it painfully whacked the instep of his left foot.

After a doctor from the club had examined the injury–he finally swung his driver and hit the ball straight up, barely one hundred yards toward the rough on the right. And, it might very well have made it those hundred yards, had that breeze not come up, and ever so gently gathered his ball and pushed it back–back–back in the direction of the tee box. Everyone looked in amazement–and even scattered to get out of the way–as the ball finally plopped down, less than ten yards down the fairway.

A stream of pee flowed down McLean's left leg and filled his shoe.

––––––––––––––––

As the caddy put the flag into the tenth hole, Alice, George, the Professor, Flynn and Turner congratulated Ti while McLean–beaten and embarrassed–hurried away alone. His fans, both from Grassy Sprain and Cincinnati, had long since deserted him.

Alice had never seen a money match before, and she was beside herself as she said, "Wonderful! Ti, just wonderful. But I did feel a little sorry for Mister McLean. Am I mistaken or was he just a little off his game today?"

Flynn answered quickly, "A little off? Ten up with eight to play? For some reason, he had no game today. No game at all."

Turner smiled knowingly.

Ti looked at Alice, and said seriously, "Don't feel sorry for The Fox, Alice. It could have been him–right here–right now–picking my bones."

Alice nodded as Flynn looked at Ti shrewdly and said, "Come with me, Ti. Somebody wants to meet you."

Ti shook his head. "Not now, Leo. I'd like to but Alice and I need to get on. We've got a..."

Flynn interrupted, "Trust me, Ti. You'd better meet this guy." He smiled at Alice, and said, "We'll be back in just a minute."

Flynn led Ti over to the shade of a tree where a prosperous looking man in his sixties stood with a scowl on his face. As Ti walked up, the man gave him a hard look, and didn't wait for an introduction from Flynn, as he said, "I swore that if I came face-to-face with the sonofabitch who cost me fifty thousand dollars today–I'd do something about it."

Ti straightened up. *Great,* he thought. *Flynn brings me all the way over here to get into a fight?* He clinched his fists and prepared for battle.

Rattling his own sword, Ti said, "Oh yeah! Like do what?"

The man stepped directly in front of Ti and said, "Like shake his hand!" With a huge smile, he offered his hand. "I'm Walter Chrysler."

As they shook hands, Ti smiled and said, "Nice to meet you, Mr. Chrysler. You play golf?"

"No, but if I did, I sure wouldn't play you. I build cars," he said and then laughed admiringly. "I bet against you today. But that's the last time."

Chrysler motioned at Flynn. "I was telling Leo here, it might not hurt if I spread the word among my friends at other clubs that they ought to get their club champ to play you. Maybe I can get some of my money back."

Flynn beamed and said, "I'll be glad to work out the arrangements."

Chrysler put his arm around Ti like a son and walked him away from Flynn saying, "Now Ti, there are some other folks I want you to meet. They are as good at what they do–as you are at what you do."

―――――――

True to his word, at Lindy's that night, Chrysler introduced Ti to a big man with a big schooner of beer. Alice was at Ti's side as Walter Chrysler said, "Ti, I want you to meet The Babe. Babe Ruth."

Ruth was a mountain of a man with a huge belly which he couldn't seem to fill. But he tried as he ate, drank and talked–all at the same time. "Hey, Keed! Any time you want to see the Yankees play–just let me know," said Ruth. He looked at the awe struck Alice and was impressed as he said to Ti, "You are a lucky man." He put his arm playfully around Ti's neck in a semi-bear hug and dragged him away to meet someone else.

Alice was left behind, fighting to get through the crowd and follow.

The Babe said to Ti, "Ever met a real thespian?"

Ti, thinking he said lesbian, asked, "A what?"

"Thespian! – thespian! An actor! This is John Barrymore. Great actor. Look at the honker on this guy."

Barrymore feigned indignity for a long, posed moment. Finally, still in character, he said, "I prefer to call it a great profile."

The Babe slapped his own huge stomach with both hands. "And I prefer to call this a powerful build." Everyone laughed, no harder than the Babe himself.

As Alice finally managed to elbow her way through the crowd, she suddenly found herself standing directly beside The Great Barrymore. It seemed like her prayers were being answered as he kissed her hand and said, "My dear. My dear. You are without a doubt–the quintessential vision of loveliness."

A photographer with a camera worked his way through the milling crowd. *Boy oh boy*, he thought. *Ruth, Barrymore–the never photographed Titanic–and even a great looking dame!* He quickly loaded the camera, and said, "Smile!" Quickly Barrymore struck a pose. Then motioned to Ruth and Ti, "Come, come gentlemen! Never disappoint a member of the fourth estate."

Ti was quickly manhandled by Ruth and inserted in the middle of the shot–but just as quickly, Ti extricated himself and raised his hands to cover his face before the camera went, click.

Barrymore was totally puzzled. "Problem? My good man?"

Ti was as serious as sin when he said coldly, "Publicity is something I don't want or need in my business."

Barrymore was confused. "Oh? But–why?"

Ruth figured it out first and said, "Hell John, this is the guy they call Titanic."

Barrymore still drew a blank.

"You know. The golfer who beat McLean in that big money match this afternoon!"

"And that's a secret?" said Barrymore.

"Well it ain't on the sports page 'cause it's gamblin'," said Ruth.

Barrymore feigned shock. With the back of his hand to his forehead, he instinctively played to the crowd with, "A victory and no reviews? My God! How depressing!"

The admiring crowd around him roared. Then Barrymore lowered his voice and dropped his act as he spoke quietly, sincerely, almost apologetically to Ti. "A gambler! Well, I must admit, I do like that. One must take risks in my business as well."

Ruth saw the genuine admiration for Ti in Barrymore's eyes, as he said, "Ti's the best at figurin' any proposition. And he'll bet any amount of money he can do it–figure it out–or know when it's gonna happen."

Barrymore was both impressed and puzzled, "When what's going to happen?"

"Anything! And he wins!" Ruth said. He tapped his head. "He's got it."

Barrymore thought for a second, then lapsed back into his more comfortable role as actor. With a Shakespearian finger in the air, he said, "To wit! You call the money–you call the game. I'll call the winner–Titanic's his name."

He bowed several times as the crowd of admirers applauded. *What else can possibly happen?* Alice wondered as Ti ushered her toward the front door.

Chapter 14

It Was Just a Feeling, But–

The next few weeks were just a blur not only to Ti, but also to his support group–Alice, Flynn, George, the Professor and now, the reporter, Turner.

Weeks later, they would all look back and remember–not each match–but the whole series of matches that seemed to all blend into one memory. A wedge shot here. A beautiful low hook there. A sandie when he had to have it. A tremendous drive.

But the one most unforgettable thing they all remembered, was the very last day, on the very last hole, when Ti absolutely had to make one of those nasty, downhill, twenty-five foot putts to beat Bud Granger from Sagamore Country Club–and he did.

The truth was, Bud was not only a lot better than Flynn imagined, but also Bud took special precautions. He had heard that Ti had a way of screwing your mind around, so he stayed, locked in the caddy shack, until tee-off time. During the match, Bud never spoke one word to Ti, or allowed Ti to speak to him–until it was over. Something like one hundred and seventy-five thousand dollars was on the line that day–between Flynn and Ti and all the others–and Ti did feel some pressure. In fact, he made a couple of bad shots–for him.

But, the Professor had it figured right. Take the good when it falls in your lap, but be prepared for the worst–because it won't be far behind. And even after he had won that last, tough day–after he had made that great putt to win–Ti still had a nagging feeling that something–somewhere out there–was turning out the wrong way for him. *Where do I get these crazy feelings, anyway?* he wondered.

And even as Walter Chrysler smiled and celebrated the victory and his winnings along with Flynn, the Professor, George, and of course, Alice and her new friend, the peanut-eating *New York Times* reporter, Turner–Ti still had that strange, dull feeling way down in his gut that something just wasn't working right.

He had lived off his wits long enough to trust those Arkansas instincts which had served him so well and for so long. No. Even with all the good things happening right then, Ti knew something was wrong.

He was, of course, right. Because carefully

standing well out of sight all day–hidden far back in the crowd–was a thoughtful Gerald St. James. One look at his sullen face and anyone would immediately see that Gerald had a problem. A big one. And, Gerald's problem had played a little too well that day–and won far too much money.

St. James hobbled away on his cane, deep in thought, as on the eighteenth green, Alice was giving Ti a big hug and a kiss, while Flynn, the Professor, George and Turner all looked on ecstatically.

Flynn was almost ready to send Turner away when Turner said, "Flynn. I'm on your side! I swear! No publicity. Okay? I'm just a fan. A big one!"

Flynn smiled and nodded. He motioned and a waiter popped the cork on a big magnum of champagne. Everyone, except Ti, filled a glass, raised it high in the air, and yelled, "Hooray!" Turner said with unabashed adulation, "To the only unsinkable Titanic!" Then, everyone yelled again, "Hoooorrrraaay!"

But–this did not please the Professor. His eyes narrowed. Unnoticed, he passed on the toast and exchanged a knowing look with Ti.

They hoped the toast would not become a curse.

Chapter 15

To Wed
Or Not To Wed?
That's The Question.

That night, arm and arm, Ti and Alice walked slowly down Broadway, going nowhere in particular. The lights from the theaters and restaurants flickered off their faces as Alice looked at Ti and said, "I meant to tell you–"

"Yeah?"

"The day you won me for the month–that was pretty good stuff."

"You liked that, huh?"

"Yes. It's been a good month. But the way you did it. You just came up with that bet in your mind–got Jack to agree to it–"

"With a little help."

"But you did it. Right then and there. Yes. That was pretty good stuff." She looked puzzled for a moment, then continued, "But what if I hadn't agreed? What if I'd just said–no way Jose."

Ti smiled. "Had it all figured, Alice. A good-looking, smart woman, like you–she isn't going to spend the rest of her life with some blue blood like Jack St. James. He'd bore you to death."

"Maybe." Alice said, smiling. She was enjoying the analysis. "But then–after the bet was made–you still had to walk right up to that golf ball and actually hit it straight into the hole."

"Sure." Ti said casually.

"Ti. Most people just can't do that. What if you'd missed?"

"Never considered that possibility."

"But–that's just hard to do."

"It's the way I am. The way I do things, Alice. I just think it through–all the way through–make up my mind to do it, and then I just do it."

"You make it sound so easy."

"Not easy at all. And the thinking is the hardest part. Not the doing." Ti said seriously. "No different than asking someone to marry you."

Alice was all ears as she said, "It's not?"

"No. The first thing you have to do is ask yourself all the right questions."

"Such as?"

"Such as–do Alice and I get along? Yep. Do we like the same things? Yep. Do we want the same things?" He looked at her. "By the way–I want to be a millionaire, belong to a fancy country club and play golf. That all right with you?"

"Yep," she said imitating him.

He smiled and continued, "Then you ask

yourself more questions–like does she understand that I need a lot of loose rein?" He looked at her a long moment.

"Yep." Imitating him again.

"And, does she understand that until I make enough money, hotels–and not staying in one place too long–is the way I have to live."

Alice knew this was important, and she dropped her carefree tone and turned dead serious as she said for the record, "A house can wait."

They both stopped walking and turned toward each other, as Ti said, "But, most important, if I asked her to marry me, what would be the odds on her saying yes–right then and there? I mean, nobody wants to hear–no way, Jose."

"Ti, there's no way I'd say–no way Jose–to that role. The odds are good, Ti. Real good. In fact," she put her arms around his neck and said tenderly, " I'd call it a sure thing." They kissed.

Then Ti said with great sincerity, "Alice, you need to be real sure. You are sure you really want to do this?"

Alice was nearly in tears as she answered with absolute conviction, "Oh, yes. Yes I..."

―――――――――

"I do," Alice said happily–and with that, the minister said, "I now pronounce you man and wife."

And so it was there, in a small New York City chapel, that Ti and Alice concluded their wedding ceremony. Ti slipped a ring on Alice's finger, and as they kissed, George, the Professor, Flynn, and Turner all crowded around the newlyweds offering their congratulations.

———————————

That evening, as Ti and Alice happily entered The Plaza Hotel, Frank, the desk clerk, was chatting on the telephone. He looked up and saw Alice rushing up to him with Ti. She stopped and gushed, "Frank! I live here–I mean I really live here."

Frank said sincerely, "Good for you, Alice. Good for you." He watched as Ti and Alice happily reached the elevator, and went inside just as the door closed.

Frank returned to his phone conversation, and with a look of devilish glee, spoke into the receiver and said, "Yes, Mr. St. James. Just today. You didn't know. Well, my oh my!"

On the other end of the phone, at a table on a balcony with a breathtaking view of the New York skyline, sat Jack St. James, trying his best to hide his utter dismay, even from himself. On the table was a cup of coffee, a plate with pastries, and a calendar with all thirty days–finally marked off.

Around the corner, just inside the apartment,

Jack's gentleman's gentleman, Davenport, was eavesdropping, as Jack said into the phone, "Uhhh–well, of course! Certainly I knew Alice was getting married. Please–yes please give her–and of course Mister Thomas–my most sincere, most heartfelt congratulations! And please relate to them–both in concert and individually–that I hope they will be ever so happy."

He slammed the phone down–cracking pieces of it off–and took a very deep breath, just as Davenport eased onto the balcony, and started to tidy things up a bit. After testing the phone to make sure that–although damaged–it still worked, he swept the broken pieces into a receptacle, then he worked on the table a bit, all the while, watching Jack out of the corner of his eye.

"Begging your pardon, sir," he said quietly. "But, isn't this rather shocking news? I always assumed that Miss Alice would be the eventual mistress of this house."

There was a slight cut to Jack's voice as he answered, "Well, Davenport. It uh–does appear that the proverbial bird has–flown." Then Davenport, as if he were waiting for someone to toss him a bag of nitro, cautiously said, "Then is there anything–anything at all I can get you? A croissant, possibly?"

Jack was lost in his thoughts as he dialed another phone number. As much to get rid of Davenport as anything else, he said, "Yes, a croissant, that would be nice. With possibly the tiniest bit of orange marmalade–and maybe just a smidgeon of that strawberry cream cheese which the specialty shop downstairs does so well?"

"Certainly. Right away, sir," Davenport answered, as he made his way back to the kitchen.

Davenport paused, looked around to make sure that no one was watching–then leaned back toward the balcony to practice his most accomplished skill–eavesdropping. He heard Jack saying–in a way that seemed a little too manly, "Dad! Yes, it's Jack!"

At the same time, high above the New York skyline, near the top of the Plaza Hotel, Ti carried a thrilled Alice over the threshold of their new apartment. He put her down and watched her as she looked around the elegant room like a child in a candy store. She returned to him and whispered, "Ti, I just–I just feel like I'm on top of a world without a worry in it."

Ti smiled and pulled her close, then they kissed.

But back on Jack's balcony, things were not going so well. Jack's face was twisted in hatred as he listened on his phone and heard his father, Gerald, say, "Jack. It's all for the best. Good riddance. Promise me you will forget about her." But the old man, with a certain look added, "But now–as far as that five hundred yard drive that Thomas claims to be able to do..."

Jack nearly screamed, "He'll never be able to do it."

Gerald smiled. In a condescending manner he answered, "Of course not. Of course he won't. And that's not the kind of news I would keep to myself."

Jack agreed and hung up the phone. *She may be able to forget about me–but he won't*, he thought bitterly.

Early the next afternoon at Clancey's speakeasy, New York's most sports-smart place to drink, things were a little slow. So, Clancey accepted a few dollars from a patron, looked around carefully, handed him a slip of paper, then said quickly while ushering him away, "Okay. Okay! You drive a hard bargain, but two to one it is. You're covered."

Sure, Clancey would take a bet or two, but he didn't work hard at it. Instead, he did the smart thing and left almost all of that to the hoodlums who ran the numbers racket, prostitution and such in the neighborhood. He was content to happily work behind the bar, and he was doing that very thing–in fact, drying glasses–as two regulars, Ivins and Turner from *The New York Times*, staggered in–dry, depleted and much the worst for wear.

Clancey glanced at his watch, and said, "In a

little bit early today, aren't you boys?" He quickly poured their usuals, then shoved them down the bar top to them, just as they collapsed on their bar stools.

"Yeah, well, things are a little slow," Turner said, as he took a drink.

"Well, I'm sure a couple a news hounds like the two of you will turn something up," said Clancey with little sincerity.

Clancey had no idea that the next man who would walk into his establishment would indeed have news for them. For it was Jack St. James who–after making a grand entrance–said brightly to the two reporters, but loud enough for all to hear, "Hello! Fancy meeting the two of you here!"

Turner and Ivins turned to see the dapper Jack St. James jauntily walking over to them as he said, "As a matter of fact, you two men of the fourth estate just might be interested in some information I have."

With a smirk, Turner said, "Afraid not, Jack. We don't cover formal occasions."

Ivins countered with, "Yeah, St. James. We follow bloodhounds, not blue bloods."

St. James waited until the considerable laughter–which had spread from their little group to the entire place–had subsided. Then he said haughtily, "My. What a shame! I just thought you might possibly be interested in an exclusive story about a nondescript fellow I met recently. Now, what was his name?"

"How about Reginald? Or maybe Ferdinand?" Turner said, eyeing Ivins for support.

Nearly gagging on his drink, Ivins managed to get out, "What about Fauntleroy?"

"As in Little Lord?" said Turner, laughing–nearly falling off his stool.

The two reporters dissolved into almost uncontrollable laughter.

With a studied delivery, St. James said, "No, I believe they called him something more quaint, something like Humongous–or Colossal–or was it Gigantic? Or possibly it was–yes! That's it! It was Titanic!" he said with that strange combination of both bitterness and happiness that only a desperate person–aching to hurt someone–ever feels.

Turner and Ivins, both good reporters, could see that bitterness, not very well hidden, in St. James's eyes. While they did not like or admire it, still they did as they had done so often in their careers–they quickly changed gears and attitude. For even considering the source, this just might be news.

"You mean Titanic, the golfer?" Said Turner intently, pretending it might not be.

"The one and only Titanic–the hustler?" said Ivins.

And St. James was loving every second. "Come to think of it–it was Titanic. *The* Titanic.

The one and *only* Titanic–as you put it," said St. James mockingly, and with complete satisfaction.

"Oh, man! Now, if you've got a story about Titanic, that is different, Jack. Old buddy. Old pal!" said Ivins, as he winked at Turner, and quickly offered St. James a seat.

Always playing the gentleman, St. James said, "Thank you. Now, the other day, I..."

Turner was in no hurry to hear it all, so he decided to delay the inevitable by interjecting, "Titanic. Man! In a world full of everything I've already seen and heard, finally, one interesting guy!" And for awhile, the ploy seemed to be working.

Ivins, urged on by Turner, totally forgot about St. James and chimed in, "One of a kind. Mind like a steel trap."

"Yeah. A trap for fools," said Turner as he motioned for Clancey to pour Ivins another drink.

"Whatever!" said St. James. He wanted to get on with his story, but Turner cut him off again, saying, "You know, I've heard he can get maybe ten side bets going in a single hand of cards. Everybody else gets so confused they lose their concentration."

"And their money!" said Ivins, taking a drink and totally forgetting St. James.

Turner eyed the steaming St. James, and quickly added, "Not Ti. The trick is, he doesn't have to write down a damn thing! He's got it all right up there." He pointed at his forehead, and both reporters laughed.

Ivins had a brainstorm. He remembered a column he had always wanted to write. He raised his finger and said as if reciting, "Put him in the middle of chaos, and he will bring order, then turn it to his advantage!"

Just as Turner was ready to follow with his own quote, St. James brought the curtain down. He was now onto Turner's game and struck back loudly and quickly.

He grabbed Ivins by the lapels, and said with a wild, almost crazed look, "This is not a fucking Titanic fan club meeting! Have either of you two seen Titanic hit a golf ball five hundred yards? No!–you have not! Because he can not!"

There was complete silence for a second. Then, Ivins took out his pencil and pad and said, "I smell a story."

Turner chose rather to order another drink.

St. James maniacally started to pace Clancey's floor as he continued, "A story? Yes! A story of deception, braggadociousness and an overinflated ego." He turned directly to Turner and said, "Why, the man you seem to admire so much, is no better than his bogus claim that he can hit a golf ball five-hundred yards!"

St. James lowered his voice and looked Turner square in the eye. "Titanic is the worst kind! A fake! A phony! And, most of all, a liar!"

Stunned, Turner said, "Those are mighty strong words when you're talking about a man of Titanic's abilities."

Ivins agreed and said, "St. James. You'd better be careful. A considerable amount of money has been lost betting against him, specially with that kind of attitude."

Turner looked like a cold glass of water had been thrown in his face. *Wait a minute,* he thought. *I wasn't born yesterday.* He took a stern look at St. James and got ready to pin him down, once and for all. "Now come on, St. James. You really mean you are telling us that Ti is willing to bet you he can hit a golf ball five-hundred yards?" Turner looked at Ivins for support. "Bet it's a joke. He'll probably hit it down a road. Yeah. That's it! It's all a big damned joke."

"Joke, hell!" St. James shouted. "And it won't be down any man-made road. That would be nothing but chickenshit! I'm too smart to let him get away with that! No! The bet is five-hundred yards! From–directly from–the fourteenth tee box at Long Island Country Club! And yes, with a golf club, not a cannon! It was clear!"

There. It was all out there now, St. James thought with a contentment he had never known. He had clearly described the bet. Exactly how Thomas said he would do it. Exactly where he would do it–and the nitwit newspaper boys got it all.

"Say, how much was the bet for?" asked Turner, still skeptical.

"Good question! Excellent question," said St. James. "And, by the way, I am now ready to call his bluff and accept his bet in front of all of you, my witnesses. The bet is going to cost Titanic one-hundred thousand dollars, and better still, his reputation. And you may print this!"

Even Turner took out his pad and pencil as St. James continued, "Yesterday, in an opulent, upscale restaurant he frequents with the social elite, Jack St. James said that he was more than confident that when history recalls the cheap hustler, once known as Titanic, it will be recorded that..."

The next morning, in their bedroom in The Plaza, Ti, wearing a silk bathrobe, sat calmly at a serving table, casually eating a breakfast of steak, salad and ice cream.

Alice was still in bed, and visibly upset as she read aloud from the morning newspaper, the part which quoted Jack as saying, "...And so, the great Titanic proved to be nothing more than a liar– a cheat–a blow hard who went the way of all deceitful braggarts after recklessly letting his monumental ego–"

She was so mad, she had to stop. But Ti said, "Okay–go on, my monumental ego, what was that,

Alice?"

"Uh–his monumental ego–uh–blind him to his own severe inadequacies..."

She looked to see if Ti was mad. He was not, and that upset her even more. She threw the paper down and glared at Ti as he just continued to eat, peacefully.

Seething, Alice almost screamed, "I can't believe it! You work so hard. And now Jack seems hell bent on destroying your reputation." She waited for a reply. Or, any sign of emotion. There was none, so she added numbly, "Aren't you mad, at all?"

Ti calmly said, "You bet I'm mad! I mean some things just aren't right! Sometimes, you just got to get bare-knuckled-tough in this world, right Alice?"

"That's right. Thata boy!" she said. *Now that's more like it. Give 'em hell, Ti,* she thought.

Ti's anger was visibly growing as he said, "I mean, damn! This is a pretty swell hotel, right Alice?"

"You bet it is!" She agreed, though not having any idea what he meant by that.

"And what really makes me mad..."

Yes, yes, she thought. *Let's hear it!*

"What really makes me mad is when I distinctly order chocolate ice cream–and what do they send up? Strawberry! Oh, I can eat strawberry, but it is not what I ordered. Not at all. And that really–and I mean really makes me mad!"

She got it. He was playing games with her. And that didn't help things. She was worried so she said, "Ti, we're talking about a one-hundred thousand dollar bet here. What are you going to do about that? Let's get him!" she said as she pumped her fist in the air.

"Don't worry, Alice, I've got six months to figure that out. When I'm ready–and I mean good and ready–I'll hit a golf ball five hundred yards from the fourteenth tee at the Long Island Country Club."

She looked around and took mental note of his playing cards, dice, golf clubs, golf balls and .45 revolver–all strewn casually around the hotel room. She shook her head and said numbly, almost to herself, "You're absolutely right, Ti. It's just a normal day."

Chapter 16

Notso Smart
After All.

It was daylight, but Ti and Alice were still in bed. Ti was half asleep, but Alice was wide awake, and staring at the ceiling as she said, "Know what I'd really like for a wedding present?"

Groggily, Ti barely mumbled, "Uhh. Uhh."

"I'd really like to help you work a proposition. Nothing big, mind you. Just something easy. What do you say? Okay?"

"Uhh. Uhh."

"Oh, come on. It would be fun."

Ti was waking up a little more now. He didn't like this subject. "Fun for you, maybe, but not for me. I don't work with amateurs."

That did it. Alice was hot as she said, "Amateurs? Me? An amateur? I am–in case you've already forgotten–an actress, a trained professional actress! You should know, you've seen me on the screen!"

Ti rolled over and looked at her. He wanted

to get this straight–once and for all. "Look, I don't want you involved in that kind of thing," he said with finality.

"Come on. Ti," Alice said, almost pleading. "What could it hurt, just once?"

Ti rolled back over. "Sorry, Alice. The answer's no. Absolutely not. End of discussion."

Steaming, Alice got up, stomped into the bathroom, and slammed the door.

Ti just shook his head. *Actresses!* he thought.

———————

There is always a price you pay to have honesty in a relationship, and Ti seemed to still be paying that price later that night at Rizzo's Italian Restaurant. At least that's the way it appeared to George as he entered the restaurant and saw Ti and Alice, already seated at a table, and obviously well into a very serious argument. As George walked up to their table, he heard a perplexed Ti say, "That's just not right, Alice. That just can't be."

When she saw George standing there, Alice said brusquely, "Ti. Not in front of George!" Then she tossed her napkin down on the table, and added, "Maybe I can have a more intelligent conversation with Mister Fuqua over there!"

A stunned Ti and George watched as Alice, in a huff, got up from the table and walked directly over to Notso Fuqua, who was sitting alone at a table across the room. Ti called after her, "Mister Fuqua?"

Ti could only shake his head as, to his further embarrassment and outright amazement, Alice sat down at Notso's table and began an animated discussion.

Ti appeared truly bewildered as he looked at George, and said, "It's funny, George. You think you know someone before you marry her. Then you marry her–and a week later you wonder if you ever knew her at all?"

But George was only casually listening. He was more intent on trying to make eye-contact with a blonde who was prominently displaying her ample cleavage from across the room. "Aw, lovers' quarrel," he said to Ti while winking at the blonde. "Forgive and forget."

"Oh–I can forgive–but I can't forget how stupid Notso is. Right, George? Isn't that a fact?"

"Well, sure, everybody knows that."

"Not Alice. She thinks Notso is one of the smartest men she's ever met."

That got George's attention. In fact he was stunned as he repeated, "Smart? Notso Fuqua–smart? She's got to be kidding!"

"Nope. She's not. I can't convince her otherwise. Say, you want to try?"

George laughed and said, "Why not! Shouldn't be too hard."

"Good," Ti said as he got up from the table and nodded over at Alice and Notso. "Come on."

George followed Ti as they walked directly over to Notso's table. They arrived just in time to hear an enthralled Alice say, "So, you feel that Shakespeare is not dissimilar to Thoreau, in that their imagery is far more important than their narrative?"

Notso shook his head like a robot and said, "Yeah."

"That's incredibly interesting. I've never heard it put quite that way before! You've given me a totally new perspective," she said, deep in thought.

Ti and George looked at each other skeptically. Ti said, "Alice, George wants to talk to you for just a minute." Alice nodded with a little too much formality, then got up from the table saying, "Excuse me, Mister Fuqua. Hold that thought."

Alice, Ti and George all took a few steps away from the table where Ti took her firmly by the arm and said, "I asked George here to talk a little sense into you."

George nodded and said, "Now, I don't mean to get in the middle of a family dispute, but Alice–with all due respect–Notso Fuqua can't count from one to two."

Alice answered defensively, "Mathematically, he may very well have problems. Many geniuses do."

George was thunderstruck as he repeated, "Genius?"

"Yes. I consider Mister Fuqua to be a genius in linguistics." She quickly saw that George had never heard the word. "You know–words! The study of words!" And that was it. Both Ti and George burst out laughing.

Ti rubbed it in. "Words? You mean the kind with letters in them?" George was getting a little uncomfortable. People were starting to watch–and anyway, he genuinely hated to see a problem like this so early in their marriage.

Ti didn't help matters, when with tears in his eyes from laughing, he said, "Come on, Alice. He can't even spell his own name!"

That did it. Now the fat was in the fire. A boiling mad Alice poked Ti in the chest and said, "And I'll bet you five-hundred dollars he can spell words you can barely pronounce! Come on big shot, five-hundred dollars!"

With the subject of money being thrown around, Ti's eyes narrowed as he just shook his head and said, "Smart. Real smart, Alice. You know you got nothing to lose when we're betting out of the same bankroll."

That was just what George was waiting to hear, and he quickly offered, "Well, Ti. Now if she weren't betting your money, I'd sure as hell take her up on that proposition."

Ti thought a second then said, "Normally, I wouldn't throw away good money. But George, she needs to learn a lesson."

"Then, you wouldn't mind?"

"You'd be doing me a favor."

George turned to Alice and with a relieved smile, said, "Okay, Alice, you got a bet." He hesitated, then continued, "But–I get to pick the word. Now let's see. Uhhh–oh, hell! What difference does it make? Mother! Just tell him to spell Mother!"

"Oh, no, George McGuire!" She said sternly. "We won't have any of that!"

George was lost. "Any of what?"

"An easy word like that won't prove a thing. Let's say it has to be at least a ten letter word. Is that fair?"

"Uh–yeah–well, okay. Well, sure!" *What the hell difference does it make what he tries to spell?* he thought.

Alice said, "All right then, George. Just name a ten-letter word." George thought a minute, but nothing came to him.

Impatiently, Alice said, "Any one will do." Embarrassed, George as much as admitted he was completely stumped, as he looked pleadingly at Alice and mumbled, "I, uh..."

Alice looked around the room as she said, "We need some help here." She spotted a spectacled gentleman who had just entered the restaurant and was headed their way.

"That guy all right?" she said as she pointed him out to George, who answered quickly, "Sure. Why not?"

Alice spoke directly to the gentleman as he walked by. "Pardon me, sir. May I ask what you do for a living?"

He was mildly irritated that she would ask, but answered, "If you must know, I'm an attorney."

"Perfect," she said. "You see, we were having a little discussion here and we need your help."

"Oh, I really don't have the time. I..."

"I know this sounds crazy, but it's very important for us to think of a few words with ten letters or more. If you'll help us, we'll be more than happy to buy your dinner," she said as she looked to George for approval–and got it.

The gentleman's tone changed, "Well, in that case–okay then." She gave him a pencil and paper and he sat down at Notso's table.

As he wrote, they all looked over his shoulder. Everyone except Notso. The attorney made little noises as if he were counting the letters. Then he wrote the first word, Cacciatore. More mumbling, some head scratching, then he scribbled the second word, Rhinoceros. Not much waiting for the third word, Restaurant. But the fourth word was real pain and agony. But, finally, he wrote Mississippi.

"I'm sorry. That's all I can think of," he said, mentally exhausted.

George frowned, and said, "That's all? That's it?"

Alice whispered to George, "That's four more than you thought of."

George nodded and said to the attorney, "Thanks a lot, pal. Send your dinner tab over to me." The attorney nodded his thanks, then retired to his table. George took the pencil and started to carefully study the list, saying, "Okay–Cacciatore. No good. Hell, it's right there on the menu." He scratched it off the list.

His pencil paused at Rhinoceros, then moved on. Looking over his shoulder, he saw RESTAURANT spelled backwards on the front window. With a smile, he quickly struck it off the list. The last word was Mississippi. His pencil traveled the path between Mississippi and Rhinoceros–several times. Then, it hesitated and finally circled–Rhinoceros.

George smiled and said to Notso, "Okay, Mister Fuqua. For five hundred bucks, let's hear you spell–Rhinoceros!"

"Rhinoceros? Sure!" said Notso as he closed his eyes and prepared himself.

Strangely, Ti and Alice looked at each other with satisfaction. Small smiles revealed that the two had something up their sleeves. Alice even looked over at the "attorney" and they exchanged huge smiles and knowing winks. Something had been meticulously planned and executed.

Then she looked back at Notso, the picture of confidence. Alice closed her eyes, her lips, ready to form the letters of the word Rhinoceros. Notso opened his eyes and repeated the word to be spelled, Rhinoceros. Then he said each letter, both confidently and carefully. "M–I–S–S–I–S–S–I–P–P–I."

For a moment, no one said a word. Finally Alice and Ti looked at each other and Alice threw her head back and burst into laughter. Incredibly, even a fifty-fifty chance, meant Notso had no chance at all.

George quickly caught on. It all had been an elaborate hoax. A scam that had backfired. Good-naturedly, he joined Alice's laughter.

The so-called attorney staggered over laughing. George gasped for breath, and tried to rub it in. "You two should have known..." but George was laughing too hard to finish. Instead, he was barely able to seat himself at the table where he buried his head in his arms and continued to laugh until he cried.

Like George, Alice was out of control. She staggered to the chair next to George, and sat down. Spent. All the while, Notso sat alone–not even understanding the joke–with a puzzled look on his face. *What's everybody laughing for. I spelled it right–didn't I?* he was thinking.

George–finally in control–said, "You two love birds should have remembered what Ti taught me. In any proposition, no matter what kind of edge you got going, there's always a certain amount of risk."

Strangely, Ti was not laughing. With a sour look on his face, he said glumly, "I really don't know what is so damn funny, Alice. Under different circumstances, I might have put some big money on a deal like this."

Then Alice looked at George, and they both erupted in laughter all over again. Alice finally blurted out, "Ti–this was just fun–just a game."

Ti shook his head sadly, "Maybe for you, but not for me. This could have been business."

At the same time, Jack St. James was in his apartment and on the phone with his father, who sat comfortably in his spacious den at the expansive St. James mansion in Long Island.

Gerald said, matter-of-factly into the phone, "Anyway, son–you really need to focus on your golf. And by the way, I've been thinking. Why not let someone else represent our club in the match against Thomas?" He paused a moment for the thought to sink in. "You might as well head on down to Florida and get some more instruction from Bob Hawkins in Miami. The Transcontinental Tournament will be coming up soon, you know, and you'll need to be at the top of your game."

"Hell no. I'm playing! I'm going to play that hustler, Thomas, and bring him to his knees, once and for all," said Jack a little too confidently.

"Sure you will," answered Gerald, with an unseen worried look on his face.

It was night, as two well-matched competitors, Gerald and Ti, sat across from each other in Gerald's cavernous den. Ti drank coffee, as Gerald sipped his favorite twenty year-old brandy from a pewter goblet with the ornate St. James crest etched on it.

Gerald lit a huge, expensive looking cigar, puffed on it to get it going, then contentedly inhaled and blew almost perfect smoke rings, which he aimed away from Ti and at a golf trophy sitting on a shelf to his left. Each nearly perfect ring encircled the little statuette which adorned the top of the trophy, on which had been inscribed, "First Place Winner–Long Island Invitational." Beneath that was the date, "1907."

Between those smoke rings, he studied Ti closely. Gerald was like an old river of molasses as the words began pouring slowly off his tongue.

"You and I are both men of the world. Different worlds, for sure. But still–we know things–how things work. And what it really takes to get things done. I had to learn because I had precious little ever given to me. I can tell it was the same way with you."

Ti looked genuinely interested. "How?"

"That twenty-foot putt on the eighteenth green, against my son, Jack–with all the chips down. Everybody watching. I was too. You don't make that kind of putt with your putter," he said as he tapped his chest. "No. It's with your heart."

He looked at Ti a long moment, partly in appreciation of what he had seen–and partly because of what he had just said. "I'd bet you even made sure you were further from the hole than Jack–so you could putt first and put the pressure on him. Right?"

Ti neither spoke nor nodded. This was St. James's show.

"Damn you. You knew you'd make your putt, right? And he wouldn't."

Ti smiled knowingly, but still said nothing as Gerald continued. "Don't get me wrong. I'd do the same thing–hell, I've done the same thing." Gerald motioned to the many trophies on the shelf beside him. "I wasn't always old. Before I hurt my leg–used to be a pretty good golfer–won the club championship a few years running."

Then, the serious, paternal side of Gerald surfaced. "I wish Jack was more like me–and hell, I'll admit it. More like you, too. But, he's not. That's why–when I can–I try to stack the deck in Jack's favor."

He took a puff from his cigar and paused for effect. "Sometimes he knows." He took a sip of brandy. "Sometimes he doesn't. And, this is one of the times I don't want him to know." Then sternly, he said quickly, "I don't want anybody to know what we discuss here today. And, I want your word on that."

"You've got it."

Gerald smiled. He needed that pledge. It pleased him and he said so. "I'll take the word from a man like you–who gambles for a living–over any other. Your word is everything in your business."

Ti nodded.

"An independent sort like yourself may think I'm a little over-protective. But have you ever known a father who didn't try to help his own son?"

"I knew one."

Gerald studied Ti and immediately understood, but did not pursue that. "Well then–try to put yourself in my place. I know that right now, Jack needs to build a little confidence in his golf–and himself. He has the chance–a damn good chance–to become the finest golfer on the East Coast–as long as he doesn't run into you again." He waited a very long moment before he said the next thing, for it was the reason why he had to have that pledge of secrecy. "Too much pressure at this stage of his development, and well–you understand."

Sure Ti understood. He nodded and said, "So–what are you getting at?"

When it came to cutting a deal, the old man

didn't mince words. "It gets down to this. In a collision course with you, Jack will lose–every time. He doesn't know that, but it's true. I don't want that to happen."

Gerald got up–supposedly just to get another drink. *The old boy doesn't miss a trick,* Ti thought. *Psychological bullshit, standing taller than your adversary. It's worked for you before, Gerald. But not today.*

Gerald even seemed to limp a little more as he made his way back to his chair, gingerly sat down and continued. "I'll do anything to make sure a match between you two doesn't happen. Ever. Understand–I will do whatever it takes to protect my son–and I will–barring an act of God."

Ti shrugged as he broached the obvious. "St. James. If Long Island Country Club sends Jack up against me, there's nothing I can do."

"Sure there is. You understand. So, what do you want? How much would it take? What gift can I offer you?"

"I'm no saint, but I don't lay down for anybody," Ti said coldly and without the slightest hesitation.

That brought Gerald up, out of his chair and onto his feet, and he was mad. "Then, from this day forward, consider Long Island Country Club, and each and every other country club on the East coast, off limits–permanently."

It was Ti's turn to show anger as he spat out,

"We'll see about that."

With a knowing look, Gerald smiled a wicked smile and said, "There is absolutely nothing to see about." He handed Ti a piece of paper. "I have the signature of every club president in the East Coast Club Association. Sometime this evening, each and every club will introduce–and carry–the motion that you are not welcome."

Stunned, Ti saw the list was both legitimate and complete, down to the last detail. "They can do that?"

Gerald summed it up nicely and legally. "Private property. Private clubs. And if you're thinking about enlisting the help of Chrysler, or anyone else–forget it. No one man gets his way."

"You damn sure seem to! Let me guess. Since I can't play on the courses anymore–I have to forfeit the rest of my matches. That makes Jack the odds on favorite to win..."

Gerald beamed as he finished the sentence for Ti, "... As well as the East Coast Club Association's representative in the winter tournament on the West coast."

"Got it all figured out, huh?"

"I'm just protecting my own. And if you have any ideas of fighting this–don't. Try, and you'll find out that you don't even know the meaning of confrontation. You've never met anybody like me. If I were you, I'd just go on back to playing cards–or plucking pigeons in the two-dollar games on the public courses."

Ti simply got up and numbly walked toward the door.

In a strange, almost apologetic voice, Gerald called after him, "Believe it or not–it's nothing personal."

"It never is," Ti said, as he left–defeated.

Gerald smiled. For the first time in a long while, he was deeply satisfied.

Chapter 17

Apples
&
Oranges

A bitter, resentful Ti drove back to the city, deep in thought. *The old bastard is no different than any father, I guess. Any father but mine.*

He could have driven a shorter route back to Alice and the Plaza, but with the St. James roadblock staring him in the face, he took the longer route, and allowed himself the luxury of looking back–and maybe even feeling a little bit sorry for himself. Something his mother had warned him against.

He also knew his mother had been right about something else, too. No matter at what level you were competing, or under what circumstances, when it was all said and done, it was still just a matter of survival.

But what his mind finally locked on during that long ride home wasn't golf, or Gerald St.

James or even the lost opportunity with the East Coast Club Association. Strangely, it was Oil City, a dirty little town in Louisiana, which came to his mind and–although he had blocked that memory for a long time now–somehow, tonight, it just seemed fitting for him to relive his visit there in 1920.

Today, after his success in New York, it was hard for him to believe that he had ever even gambled in Oil City–in its dirty, dark, smoke-filled rooms lit by kerosene lamps. But when he was younger, he had played poker there and been glad to, because to him, back then, it looked like El Dorado, "the shining city of gold."

Even then, he had a lot of nerve, but very few skills with cards or dice. And he knew nothing of the odds because gaining from the Professor's knowledge was still years away, and he had never touched a golf club.

But he had received one of the biggest shocks of his young life in Oil City, in Luke's, a small, two-room shack dedicated to booze, gambling and women–not necessarily in that order.

He had been playing poker all night and had run it up pretty good on this fellow across the table– a man probably in his late forties who was drinking heavily and appeared a lot older.

Alvin decided to go for the whole pot, and everyone dropped out except the stranger across the table, who foolishly pushed all the money he had left to the center of the table–and lost.

The game over, Alvin raked in his winnings–sixteen-hundred dollars–and walked out the door. Outside Luke's, in the dirt street, the older man followed and caught up with him saying, "If you're from Rogers, Arkansas, we may have some relatives in common."

"And who might that be?"

"Well, if your name is Alvin Thomas like I heard in there, and your ma is a woman called Sarah, that would make me your daddy."

Stunned, Alvin looked at the tall, slender man in the badly-worn suit for a long moment, then said, "I am from there, and Sarah is the name of my ma."

"Son, I'm Lee Thomas and that sixteen-hundred dollars sure proves you've learned more than I ever taught you."

When were you ever around to teach me anything? Alvin thought. But he said, "Well, it is sure nice to finally see you again."

After they passed a few inane pleasantries, Alvin finally said, "You know, it doesn't seem right for me to hold sixteen-hundred dollars of my daddy's." With that, Alvin handed his winnings back to Lee.

"Oh, I get it! You think Lee Thomas is the kinda man who'll take that money–then get down on my knees thankin' ya for it!"

Lee looked indignant. "If that's what you

think, you're dead wrong!" He quickly grabbed the money. "I ain't gettin' down on my knees," he said, as he stuffed the money in his pocket. "I take what I can get, any way I can get it. And this will get me to the next town."

And then some, Alvin thought.

Lee started to walk away, but turned back. "Just so it ain't a total loss, here's sixteen-hundred dollars worth of advice. If you don't want to end up playin' penny ante poker in tank towns like this, remember–when you're gamblin', once you got 'em, don't ever let 'em off the hook."

Lee started off again, but turned back one last time, smiled almost fondly, and said, "Looking at you, I can sure tell that the apple don't fall too far from the tree."

Hell! I sure hope it does–and rolls a whole lot further, Alvin thought as he watched his father turn and vanish into the darkness–just as he had done years ago back in Arkansas.

———————

In their room later that night, Alice was worried about Ti's bleak, almost desperate mood. She had never seen him like this. Come to think of it, she had never seen anyone this bad off. He had told her all about the confrontation with Gerald. And that there was nothing he could do–nothing, except what he was doing. So she just watched him–totally depressed–sitting in a chair in the corner, mindlessly tossing playing cards–one after another–into his hat which he had tossed on the floor.

She decided to rekindle the conversation they had just aborted. "Retired? Ridiculous! You're not retired from golf!"

"I am on the East coast."

Alice would hear none of this defeatism. "Ti, it's times like this you've got to learn to say–I'm a positive person–I'm a positive person–I'm a positive..."

"Oh, I'm positive, all right. Positive if something can go wrong–it will!" he moaned.

Determined to change the subject, she walked to the window saying, "Come here. Look! It's raining!"

A sullen Ti reluctantly joined her at the window and watched the deluge which was flooding the dark street, far below. "Yep. That's rain all right," he said with neither interest nor inflection.

"I love rain. It cleanses the earth. It renews," she added as she gamely tried to interject at least some good vibes into the dark, depressing atmosphere. "And you know what, Ti? It signals a renewal for us–for all of us. A new beginning," she said as she raised the window and took a deep breath. Then she added softly, with great affection, "You can't fool me. I know it means something special to you, too."

"Damn. You're sure right about that, Alice," he said with a tinge of sarcasm that Alice either didn't hear–or didn't want to hear. He continued. "First you hear a little pitter-patter up there on the roof." Alice started to grin, and sensing her psychology was working, she urged him on with, "Yes? – Yes?"

"Pretty soon, you notice a drip–and right after that–it really starts to leak!"

"Huh?"

"Then you're talking flooded floors, wet feet, a quick case of lung-filling pneumonia, then a really slow, painful, horrible death!"

Alice shook her head at his twisted logic. This had not gone nearly as well as she had hoped. He was getting ready to start all over again, when mercifully, the phone rang. Alice hurried over to grab it, saying, "This is probably the good news we need right now."

She picked up the phone, and said brightly, "Hello!" She listened and then smiled broadly, saying, "Great! Absolutely great idea. We'll be there." She hung up the phone, grabbed Ti's hat and slapped it on his head. "Let's go! Everybody's waiting for us at Lindy's."

But, the excitement of Lindy's dissolved into

absolute misery as Ti's bleak mood engulfed everyone else at the table–George, Flynn, the Professor and Turner. Only Alice kept her upbeat attitude, but even it was getting frayed from rubbing up against the many bad attitudes it had encountered on that rainy night. Flynn and McGuire almost felt as if they were right at home–at an Irish wake.

"Talk about the well runnin' dry," said Flynn. With Ti out of the matches, it'll be one country club boy playing another country club boy." Then he added sarcastically, "Damn! What a challenge! What a thrill!"

"Well the good news is–absolutely nothing–absolutely nothing worse can possibly happen," Alice said, almost trying to convince herself. But one look across the crowded room at someone who was headed their way, and she knew things might even get a little worse yet, as she uttered a warning, "Uh oh."

Everyone at the table looked up to see a buoyant Jack St. James approaching. He had had a few too many–nothing unusual for him–as he walked directly to Ti and said too loudly, "Well! If it isn't the chap who claims he can hit a golf ball five-hundred yards!" Laughter from other tables drifted over. Always the gentleman, Jack tipped his hat to Alice, and added lustfully, "My dear, my dear. How very nice to–see you."

Turning back to Ti, Jack pointed across the room, and said, "I've been telling my friends over there what you have proposed." His three affluent friends–all over-dressed in tuxedos–smiled and waved as if on cue. Jack waved back, swayed a little, but righted himself, and continued, "But, try as I may, I cannot convince them. You see, they don't believe you any more than I do," he said, laughing hysterically.

Jack raised his voice so that everyone in Lindy's main room that night could not help but hear, and said to Ti, "I would like to announce, in front of God and witnesses, that Thomas–or Titanic–whatever name you choose to go by–I accept your bet. You must hit a golf ball five-hundred yards off the fourteenth tee at Long Island Country Club, or pay me one-hundred thousand dollars."

Jack's three friends across the room cheered and applauded, saying, "Get him Jack." –"Atta boy." – "That's the way!"– "Make him put up or shut up!" Again, there was general laughter throughout the main room.

Jack sensed that the moment was his to seize, and he quickly went for Ti's throat. "Now, Thomas. The bet is not about hitting a golf ball off some man-made surface like a street or a road mind you– it is from the tee box at the fourteenth hole at Long Island Country Club. Agreed?"

"Okay. You're on. I'll let you know when I'm

ready," Ti said with no emotion.

"Then, so be it," Jack said as he slowly drifted back to his friends' table. Passing the departing Jack–Barrymore and Babe Ruth approached Ti's table, both sneering after St. James.

Ruth spoke first, and sadly. "Everybody's sayin' you pulled out of the big money matches 'cause you were scared of Jack of St. James. Hell! I told 'em all you must have had a better reason than that. Right, Keed?"

Ti sighed, and nodded sadly. "Yeah. But it's– it's personal."

Barrymore, no stranger to intrigue having spent his life in the theatrical business, with one finger raised, like Julius Caesar, ventured–in his best Shakespearian voice, "Me thinks the vague veil of secrecy doth clothe thy countenance like a shroud."

Although nobody, except Alice, totally understood, it was Ruth who best summed it up when he said, "Huhhh?"

Barrymore smiled–put his arm around his new friend, Ti–and said, quietly and a bit mysteriously, "I figure somebody's got you by the balls and you can't say shit."

"Something like that," Ti agreed, with a sad smile.

Suddenly, two hands covered Barrymore's eyes from behind, and a familiar voice rang out, "Barry baby!" It was Margo.

Barrymore smiled and said, "Ahhhh. A touch from heaven possessing the fire of the devil." After kissing Barrymore, Margo presented herself to the table, saying, "Hi ya folks!"

"Well, it's nice to see somebody happy tonight," Alice said with some relief.

"Happy? I'm ecstatic!" said Margo. "Finally got Hauffy off on a train back to Los Angeles. I can still see him–hanging off the back of the caboose–drunk out of his mind–screaming–New York! New York! New York!"

Everyone laughed for the first time that night as Margo continued, "I hear the bootleggers ran out of gin with him here." Another laugh, then even Margo turned serious, as she looked at Ti in a strange way, and blurted out, "Look! I don't know what all this funny business is about this golf stuff– with you droppin' out and Jack St. James gonna be the big winner and all that–but if it were me, I wouldn't sit around New York feelin' sorry for myself. With winter coming on, I'd get the hell out of here and go out to California and play a round or two with Hauffy in L.A. He told me he was the president of a country club out there. 'Course, he won't play you for more than two dollars, 'cause he's a banker–at his father-in-law's bank."

Everyone nodded their understanding of her meaning.

"Thanks Margo, but I don't think so..." Ti's

voice just trailed off. *She doesn't understand the complications,* he thought.

"Hell, just an idea. Us girls get 'em occasionally, you know," she added, a little hurt he'd said no so easily, without even thinking about it. And Ti could tell she was hurt, so he quickly added, "Didn't mean it that way, Margo. Honest to God, I really do appreciate it. It's just that..." his voice trailed off again. *What can I say,* he thought.

"Just an idea. But if you do call Hauffy–and I think you should–for God's sake, don't call him at home. He takes his personal calls at his country club. You can look up the phone number. It's called El Rainier or El Rondo or something–oh yeah, it's El Rancho. That's it. El Rancho Country Club! I remember 'cause it rhymed with the name of a businessman from Mexico I once knew–Pancho," she said flattening out the "a" in Pancho and mispronouncing it as nasal "a," and thereby making it a perfect rhyme with Rancho, which she also used a flat nasal "a" to mispronounce.

At that instant, no matter how badly Margo mispronounced El Rancho–Ti, George, and Flynn thought she sounded as eloquent as Barrymore–for the same light bulb went off in their eyes. Bingo!

Chapter 18

Paying For
That Hot Time,
in The Old Town.

Two weeks before the El Rancho Winter Golf
Tournament, in a severely over-furnished, gaudily-
decorated Beverly Hills mansion, the J.T. Van
Hauffwigin family was gathered around a dinner
table big enough to feed Cox's army.

At one distant end of the table was the
formidable, Viola Van Hauffwigin, matriarch of
the family. She was grudgingly fifty-five, fat, and
overdressed for dinner, as she searched her plate–
looking first beneath her huge slab of medium-
rare, prime rib–and then finally under her extra
large, sour cream-laden, twice baked potato–to find
that last, tender, early spring pea she loved so very
much, and which had, up until that moment, eluded
her.

Around the table were seated the rest of the
Van Hauffwigin clan. The heir apparent, Marvin,
was a spectacled twelve-year-old, obviously a little

twit, who dangled his food for his dog, then pulled it back just before the poor animal could grasp it with his teeth.

On the opposite side of the table was his sister, the ugly Lucinda. Obviously descended from a wart hog, she shoveled her food–and anyone else's she could reach–into her mouth as if there was no tomorrow. And, judging by the size of her waistline and the amount of cholesterol she was ingesting, there might not be.

Finally, at the head of the table was J.T. Van Hauffwigin, himself. Subdued, meek. He was just a shell of his former New York-self. As he pecked at his food, and looked around the table in disgust, you could almost hear that one, desperate thought which kept running around in his head. *Nuuu York! Nuuu York! Nuuu York! Nuuu York!* he obsessed in his mind. And why not? Home in L.A. was not his favorite place to be.

In an adjacent room, a phone rang and Smythe, the affected, imported butler answered. "This is the Van Hauffwigin residence," he said as if he was describing the death sentence he was serving. After a moment, he announced ceremoniously into the phone, "Certainly. By all means." Then, he went into the dining room and spoke directly to J.T. saying, "Begging your pardon, sir. An urgent phone call."

"Yes! Of course. I'll take it in the library," J.T. said, too seriously, and badly masking his delight at having a chance to escape the family's feeding trough. As he got up, he told his family–not one of whom was listening–"Excuse me."

The only response he got was a loud, "Burp," from Lucinda.

He entered the study, picked up the receiver, and said, "Hello."

On the other end of the phone line was George. He sat–relaxed and smiling–in his New York apartment with his feet propped up on a table, the phone in one hand, and a glass of straight bourbon in the other. When he heard a voice on the other end of the line, he quickly said, "J.T.! This is your old pal, George McGuire. Yeah, that's right! From New York. I was just sitting around here, talking about you with a mutual friend, and I thought we'd just call and say hello!"

Van Hauffwigin had a strange feeling this would not be a conversation he would care to share with just anyone, so he quickly said, "Uh, yes! George. Uh–can you possibly hold on for just one moment, please? Thank you."

Van Hauffwigin put the phone down and quickly walked over, quietly closed the library door, then returned to the phone. "Actually, you caught me at a rather bad time. I'll be back in New York in a month or so, maybe we could..."

But George would have none of that, as he said, "J.T.! A month is too long. Way too long. I just have one little favor to ask. My best pal, Ti

Thomas–right, you met him at Lindy's–No..." he paused as Van Hauffwigin spoke, "No. It was you, J.T.! Right! That's right. You were in the conga line. Well, anyway, guess what? Ti and his wife, Alice, are making a trip to L.A. and I thought you might invite him to play in that big-money golf tournament of yours."

After George lit a cigar and allowed Van Hauffwigin time to ponder the thought, he carefully continued, "You see, the thing is, I hear you are the president of El Rancho Country Club out there. Right pal? I thought so. So, I figured it would be no problem to get Ti an invite to your golf tournament. Right?"

There was no answer–so, George took a drink, waited, then said again, "Right J.T.? J.T.? Are you there?"

Van Hauffwigin shook his head, smiled disgustedly, and said insincerely, "George, I'd love to help your friend, but the truth is, we have a very limited field. Every player must be approved and invited by the tournament committee–and after all, we already have the East Coast Club Association's Grand Champion, Jack St. James, representing your area. It would be most difficult for any club association to have two invitations."

"Oh hell!" George said, a little irritated. "Ti doesn't belong to one of those country clubs. All you have to do is use a little pull–and get him one of those at-large invitations I heard about."

"I'm afraid not," Van Hauffwigin said. "There's always a two-year waiting list for any at-large invitation." With a satisfied smile he concluded, "So, you can see–there is absolutely no way I could possibly..."

"No way?" said George, indignantly. "There's always a way. Didn't I find a way when you wanted to meet those follies girls when you were here in New York a couple of months ago? Have you already forgotten those beautiful, exciting women, J.T.?"

George listened carefully for a moment, then smiled and said, "I didn't think so. And they sure haven't forgotten you. In fact, guess who's sitting with me right now?" He listened for a second, then exclaimed, "Psychic! You're one of those damn psychics, aren't you, J.T.? 'Cause you're right! It's Margo. And here–she wants to have a little talk-talk, chat-chat with you."

George handed the phone to Margo who sat next to him on the couch. She winked at George–prepared herself for her theatrics–then spoke excitedly into the phone, "Hauffy! Is that really you? I been thinkin' about ya night and day since ya left. And don't worry, I haven't used that bubble bath you gave me with anybody else," she said with a sly grin. "Know what I'm thinkin' about doin'?"

Van Hauffwigin's eyes widened with horror as he listened to the unthinkable. Like an attorney pleading for the life of his client, Van Hauffwigin spoke with infinite care as he said, "Margo, listen carefully, very carefully. Let me urge you not–absolutely not to make a trip out here now. I haven't been feeling well lately, and the doctors don't know if I'm contagious or not."

He listened for a horrified moment, then answered, "You simply have no idea how much I appreciate your offer, but I have more than enough highly qualified nurses out here and–uh–no, my dear–uh–no, my dear–my dear, my dear–may I speak to George, please?"

When George got the phone back from Margo, along with one of her patented winks, he said, "What a guy! I knew you could do it, J.T.! I'll put them on the train tomorrow. Be sure to give me a call next time you're in New York!"

That night in their hotel room, an excited Alice hugged Ti and said, "California! Beautiful, Southern California!"

"Think of it as our honeymoon," Ti said as he and Alice formed an assembly line and began to pack the money–the several thousand dollars he had won during the difficult matches he had played several weeks ago. He tossed the stacks of neatly bound hundred dollar bills to Alice, who placed them in a carefully selected, nondescript, brown suitcase.

Chapter 19

Watch Out California.
Here They Come!

Grand Central Train Station was alive with men, women, and children, running hither, thither, and yon, while inside a compartment of a soon-departing train, a porter stored Ti and Alice's bags away. The job finished, he said with a smile, "Will that be all, Ma'am?"

"Yes, thank you," Alice answered, as she handed him a tip. He left the compartment, closing the door behind him, and Alice turned and through her compartment's window, watched Ti, George, and Flynn standing below her on the platform, talking confidentially. She noticed as George looked around carefully, put something into Ti's brown suitcase, then closed it quickly.

"Okay. You got my money and Flynn's in there with yours. It ain't a million–but it's everything we got." He thumped Ti's brown suitcase. "Leo and I agree, you just use it however you see fit."

Ti looked stunned and said, "Any way I want?"

Uncharacteristically, Flynn smiled and said earnestly, "Look. It gets down to this. You're not only the best golfer I know, you're the smartest gambler. George and I have decided to ride along with you. Win or lose."

There was a look of deep gratitude in Ti's eyes.

"And if I lose it all?"

"Hell, I said win or lose," Flynn said gruffly.

"Ti, it wouldn't be the first time we were all broke," George said. "Anyway–the hardest thing for us is not going with you–but you don't need any extra attention."

Ti really didn't know what to say, except a quick, "Thanks. I'll do my best." At a loss for more words of gratitude, he was grateful that the train started making noises that it was ready to leave. Steam hissed from beneath the train. The attached cars popped and cracked–ready to go–so Ti sprang quickly up on the stairwell, then turned, and with a sincere smile, he reached down and shook first George's hand–then Flynn's. A moment later, Ti appeared in their compartment's window–next to a smiling Alice who blew kisses of good-bye to their friends.

" 'Board. All aboard," rang out the familiar conductor's announcement as the train lurched forward with a jerk, and then slowly started to pick up speed. Alice continued to wave from the window for as long as she could see George and Leo, then when they were out of sight, she and Ti drew the window's curtain.

———————————

As the train sped at full speed down the track toward Los Angeles, Ti and Alice stood on the platform of the caboose, at the end of train. Huge snowflakes were just starting to fall as they watched the skyline of New York fade slowly into the distance. They embraced, kissed, then both looked back at the disappearing city.

"It's not often you can say good-bye to a friend and an enemy at the same time," Alice said. "What irony."

Ti nodded. He didn't even know what "irony" meant, but he knew exactly what she was saying.

The devil was probably spanking his wife that night, for although the snow continued to fall, on the horizon–back toward the bright lights of the city of New York–a full moon peeked through the clouds and revealed a flock of migrating geese.

Ti and Alice heard their melancholy cries and watched them, as they swept across the sky, etching an almost perfect V on the moon's bright surface. They were on the move, and it was a simple matter of survival which had started them on their journey.

And so it was for Ti and Alice.

———————————

After several hours, the repetitious clickity-clack of the train speeding down the tracks, and the confinement of the four walls of their compartment, had lulled Ti and Alice into an unaccustomed state of boredom. So, they had escaped their compartment and happily joined many other passengers–sitting, drinking, snacking and relaxing in the club car.

Ti and Alice contentedly played a simple game of gin, while an overly serious-looking passenger, who sat next to Ti, alternately watched Ti's hand of cards, and a small show across the car.

The show was a fat man with his shirt sleeves rolled up, who performed for a small crowd of passengers which had gathered. Without a word spoken, he delicately placed a shelled, hard boiled egg between his thumb and index finger.

With a flourish, he showed the egg to the group, then proceeded to ever-so-carefully balance it on his forehead. He reached for a shot glass full of whiskey sitting on the club car's bar, slowly moved the shot glass toward his lips, tilted the glass and swallowed the whiskey. As his finale, he quickly snapped his head forward–sending the egg high in the air, and as it fell, he reached out with his shot glass and caught the egg in it!

With a huge grin, the Fat Man collected money from the assembled crowd as they applauded his feat.

Ti noticed the passenger next to him was staring at his cards, and could see that with just one more ace, Ti would win. He said, "You're not liable to get another one of those anytime soon."

"No? I was kind of figuring I would," Ti said.

"You're dreamin' mister. No way."

"I don't know," Ti disagreed. "Seems like a good bet to me."

Hearing the word "bet," the passenger's eyes lit up. He quickly said, "Five dollars says you won't." Then he carefully took a crisp five-dollar bill out of his coin purse and put it on the table.

Ti also flipped a five-dollar bill on the table, then, with a small smile at Alice, he drew his next card, an ace. As Ti showed the card, the passenger cringed, sadly watched Ti pocket his money, then scooted over closer to Ti, and spoke confidentially.

"Look. How'd you like to get in on the ground floor of something that's gonna be big! Real big!"

"Like what?"

"A new product I've developed that will revolutionize the lighting industry."

"No kidding?" Ti said, mildly interested.

"You bet. This is a sure thing!"

That did it. That was the wrong choice of words, so Ti shook his head. He didn't even have to think about this one.

"No, thanks. Not interested," Ti said with finality.

"Look. I just need a few thousand dollars. I really think the fluorescent light bulb will be a big moneymaker!"

With his voice dripping sarcasm, Ti said, "Sure it will, pal. Sure it will."

———————

The next day, on the practice area of a Los Angeles golf course, Howard Hughes stood in front of his chauffeur, Daryl, like a drill instructor.

Daryl was not happy, as Hughes said, "Now Daryl–I got you out here because that damned movie studio is wearing me out. Hell, today, that director and lighting man took five and a half hours to put a key light on a banana! Now I can understand if it was an actress–but a banana? I swear, all I said to him was, 'Are you sure you want to spend all this time and all my money on a piece of fruit?' He screamed at me, Daryl– screamed at me, and said that it wasn't about a banana or an actress–it was about his artistic integrity. Then, he just up and left."

Hughes looked defeated. "I'm just tired of the whole damn movie thing."

"Mr. Hughes–sir," Daryl tried to get a word in, but to no avail. Hughes was on a roll.

"And you know what else, Daryl? I am even

more tired of not having a damn person to play golf with. Not one damn person! So, I intend to teach you the fine and gentlemanly game of golf, as practiced in these United States–which is to be differentiated from that English brand of golf with that small-as-shit, little piss ant golf ball they use."

"Mr. Hughes–sir. My job description never included..."

"The first thing you learn in golf, is that the word never–is never acceptable." Hughes seemed like a little child who couldn't find a playmate as he confided, "You got to bear with me 'cause it's awful hard on a man when he can't find another man to play golf with him–and maybe make a friendly wager. Hell–at least Kate'll do that."

He smiled as he thought of Kate, but he quickly caught himself, and refocused on the lesson at hand. "Now, Daryl. You just hand me that golf club and let's get started."

Unhappily, Daryl picked up the golf bag, revealing a sign which read:

EL RANCHO COUNTRY CLUB
Members Only

As Ti and Alice sped by train to meet whatever destiny awaited them in Los Angeles, back in Long Island, Gerald St. James sat at the desk in his den, deep into a phone conversation.

His ever-present cigar and brandy at hand,

he spoke solicitously into the phone. "Well that's right, Don. I didn't think you knew." He listened for a second, then shook his head with satisfaction. "That's right. His name is Thomas, and let me assure you, he is one slippery fellow. We found out the hard way, and had to take strong measures against him back here. Very strong measures, indeed."

As he listened intently, he took a deep drag from his cigar, a sip of brandy, then he smiled and said, "I applaud that. I do! And Don, believe me, I am not trying to tell you and your members what to do–but I believe you must act in a decisive manner, and act quickly!"

He listened again, and again smiled. "Exactly! I was telling Jack just the other day, we must all stand up for what we believe in before the world is given over to this type–right–right– that type. You know what I mean."

He waited a moment, then said, "You're quite welcome. And my best to the fine members at El Rancho. One of the premiere golf clubs in the country is how we refer to you–with more than a little envy, I might add. Fine. Fine. Same to you. Good-bye."

With a satisfied, thoroughly evil smile, Gerald took a sip of brandy, another drag on his cigar, and then blew a smoke ring–this one directly at his 1907 Championship trophy. As the ring almost perfectly encircled the statuette on top of the trophy, he looked at his effort approvingly, and said, "Damn you're good."

Chapter 20

We Reserve
The Right Not To–

On the night before the big tournament, expensive, mirror-polished automobiles streamed into the huge, circular driveway leading to the front of El Rancho Country Club. Valets scurried to open car doors for the beautiful people–all so elegantly dressed–who stepped out and walked leisurely through the front door of the country club. Inside the spacious, exquisitely decorated banquet room, on a wall above the head table, a large banner proclaimed:

WELCOME TO THE
EL RANCHO WINTER GOLF
TOURNAMENT

The large, wood-paneled banquet room was filled to capacity. At table after table, beautiful women and successful looking men–most smoking cigars and cigarettes–were all eating and drinking magnificently.

This was a happy occasion for all concerned, a relaxing time. But the same could not be said for J.T Van Hauffwigin, as he uncomfortably sat at a table with Ti and Alice, and nervously whispered, "Listen to me very carefully. There will be no deviating from our agreement. Not one iota! I got you into the tournament..." he looked around to make sure no one could hear, and lowered his voice. "I entered you as Alvin Thomas from Rogers, Arkansas. And while it is permissible for you to take your meals in the buffet line with the rest of the golfers–under no circumstances will you be allowed to fraternize with our members. Nor may you drop in on any other functions being held in the club."

Ti was irritated. "Well damn, Van Hauffwigin! Why don't you just go ahead and photograph us and get our fingerprints? Hell–I'm just here to play in the tournament and make a few bets."

"One cannot be too careful. I have some of my bank's biggest clients here tonight," Van Hauffwigin said looking around again. "But, your money is as good as anyone else's." He looked at his watch. "The Calcutta starts in an hour or so– right after the opening ceremonies. But remember, be careful. And please. Please! Proper decorum at all times."

Alice could stand it no longer. *This buffoon– who stunk up New York for a month,* she thought.

He is telling Ti and me how to act?

Just to put the fear of God into him, she said, "You mean I can't strip down to my panties and bra, get up on top of this table and scream, L.A.–L.A.–L.A.–L.A.? Is that what you're getting at?"

In a terrified, trembling voice, Van Hauffwigin pleaded, "Oh for God's sake. Please! Please! Don't even say that!" He got up, weak from fear. "I've got to get back to my table."

Ti and Alice turned their attention toward the head table where Van Hauffwigin took his seat next to his wife, Viola. In front of Van Hauffwigin, on the table, was a sign with his name and the title: President.

And in front of the other men seated next to him, were placards with their names and club titles. The signs read:

Charles Craven-Finch, Vice President
D.D. Cumminski, 2nd Vice President
Don Carter, Secretary-Treasurer

Sitting next to Van Hauffwigin, Alice saw a late arrival, none other than a smiling Jack St. James. In front of him, a placard had been placed which read:

Special Guest of Honor
East Coast Club Association
Grand Champion

Accompanying all the club officers were their wives, and two of them–Evelyn Carter, and Edith Cumminski–got up and headed toward the powder room. Alice watched them and noticed the door they entered.

After a few minutes, Alice said politely to everyone at their table, "Please excuse me," as she got up and headed to the powder room, smiling. She was enjoying all of this immensely. *What a beautiful place,* she thought. And what a wonderful evening it promised to be.

Inside the powder room–just before Alice arrived–a group of women were congregated, as if someone had called a meeting. As they all fixed their makeup and hair, they eagerly listened as Evelyn Carter and Edith Cumminski powdered their not-too-pretty faces and shared the latest gossip.

"Well, Don has heard from a very reliable source, that he had been nothing more than a professional gambler in New York City," Evelyn said.

Alice entered the crowded room unnoticed, just in time to hear some of Edith's last comment. She listened with the others as Edith continued, "Little more than a cheap hustler with a decent golf swing, is how I heard him described."

"Not only that, his wife was nothing more than a part-time actress in New York," Evelyn said with a knowing smile.

It started to crash through Alice's brain. *My God! They're talking about us!* She thought in horror. *Why? What have we done?*

"And–well," said Evelyn, looking around to make sure she had center stage and everyone's attention, "One can only imagine what she did with the rest of her time!"

"The rest of her time?" Edith said with a laugh. "Well, I'm sure she spent that on her back– and I don't mean doing the back stroke!"

"Oh my!" an older woman said, looking faint. The other women all laughed.

Alice was thunderstruck, getting sick. *What kind of people are these?* she thought as she tried to hide the tears streaming down her face. One thought consumed her. *Oh, God. Please get me get out of here.* Hoping no one had yet recognized her, she tried to move toward the front door to make her escape.

But she was accidentally blocked by a large woman directly in front of her, who said to Edith and Evelyn, "Those people are actually here? Have either of you met them yet?"

"Heavens, no!" shot back Edith. "We wouldn't dirty our hands on trash like that."

I've got to get out of here! Alice screamed in her mind. She was afraid someone might recognize her and the door looked like it was a mile away.

"I can't imagine how those kind of people

ever got into this club tournament!" said yet another woman.

Evelyn quickly answered, "Don't worry. Don told me, as we were coming over tonight, that the tournament committee wants to discuss that very thing. Believe me, there will be no Alvin Thomas–or whatever his name really is–in the tournament tomorrow!"

With tears rolling down her cheeks, Alice finally reached the door and bolted toward her table trying to make her way back to Ti. This beautiful new world she had stumbled into had just turned ugly.

As she made her way back to her table, all the sounds in the room seemed to be magnified. She was able to hear voices–snatches of conversation–from the tables she passed. She held her hands over her ears, but it didn't help. The ugly voices were too loud, as they said–

"... So I told Charlie–and you know what a pansy-ass Charlie is–I said, 'Charlie, if he can't make the damned payment this time, then by God, you just put the family out! Money is money!' "

"... Well, I just couldn't make up my mind between the Stutz and the Mercedes. So, I did the only practical thing. I ordered them both..."

"... It's not my kid. That's not my cream in her ice box. No, sir! She's on her own and a slut like that..."

It seemed like hours until she finally made

her way back to her table and Ti. She quickly pulled him away toward a dark corner, and still crying, she said, "Oh Ti, please! Let's just leave!"

Tenderly he brushed a tear from her cheek, and said quietly, "Not until you tell me exactly what happened."

Getting paranoid, Alice looked to see if anyone had spotted them yet. She didn't think so, so she turned back to him and snapped, "No! Take me to the hotel–now! I've kept up the good front. I've put on the happy face. I've looked for the silver lining–and now I've had it!"

This had been building in her a long while and she was determined to have her say. "I admit it! I was wrong! You and the Professor were right! Expect the worst and you won't be disappointed. Boy, were you two right!"

She bolted toward the front door with Ti right behind her. She reached the car at the same time he caught up with her, and they both got in. He angrily started the motor, gunned the car out of the El Rancho driveway, then into the dark night.

They pulled up in front of their hotel, and Ti stopped the car with a squeal. This time it was Ti in the lead, with a calmer Alice in hot pursuit. He didn't break stride until he hit the front desk where he demanded from a surprised desk clerk, "My

suitcase, damn it! The brown one! And hurry!"
Seconds later, after getting it from a walk-in safe,
the clerk handed over the suitcase to Ti, after he
had signed for it.

Even though Alice had calmed down, minute
by minute, Ti had gotten madder and madder. And
it was she, who was now running after him, as he
reached the car, and got in. She caught him just as
he was starting the motor, and she said quickly,
"What are you going to do?"

"Something I should have done a long time
ago," he said. He pointed at the front door of the
hotel. "Now get back in there!"

"But..."

"And don't you try one of those actress's
emotional reversals on me," he said, remembering
one of her acting tricks she had taught him. He
roared away leaving her on the sidewalk–but not
for long.

She quickly hailed a cab and set out in hot
pursuit.

———————

Ti headed his car into the El Rancho parking
lot a little too quickly, bounced on the entryway,
and screeched to a stop directly in front of the main
entrance. He got out, suitcase in hand, and headed
through the front door like a bull looking for a
china closet.

Alice's cab pulled up right behind him and she got out and tried to head Ti off.

"Ti, forget it!"

"You forget it, Alice. I don't want to."

"They aren't worth it!" she pleaded.

"Oh, yes they are! They're worth every penny of it," he said with a mischievous smile. "And cheer up, Alice. Things aren't that bad. In fact, I've got a feeling I'm about to get lucky."

Alice looked dumbfounded. *Lucky? He's going to get lucky?* she thought. She numbly followed him into and through the club and directly into the banquet room, where everyone was just finishing dinner.

With Alice at his side, Ti eased into a dark corner and watched as Van Hauffwigin rose from his seat of honor at the head table and tapped his water glass to quiet the eager crowd. Then he said, "Ladies and Gentlemen, I want to welcome each and every one of you to our annual El Rancho Winter Golf Tournament. This year, we are honored to have as our guest speaker, one of our participants. A man who is considered by many to be the finest golfer in this country! The world renowned, amateur golfing champion, the unbeatable, Jack St. James."

The crowd broke into spontaneous applause as Jack stood and raised his hands in false humility.

Van Hauffwigin signaled, and on cue, behind him, a banner unfurled which read:

WELCOME JACK ST. JAMES

In the audience, men's faces were filled with deep admiration, and women's faces reflected unabashed passion for this handsome champion. Jack was finally able to quiet the crowd, and when he was sure you could hear a pin drop, he started his canned pitch. "Mr. President and members. Being called the finest golfer in the country, is not something I take lightly. No. Far from it. It is, actually, even more important to me than the many, many trophies and medals which adorn my walls. In fact, I consider it such a compliment that..."

But he would never finish that sentence, for from the back of the room, a loud voice exploded, "Excuse me! Excuse me just one second, please!"

Every head turned toward the rear and every mouth whispered in disbelief at this affront. They strained to see who it was who would do such a thing, and as they looked, Ti stepped out from the darkness.

Seeing the offender clearly, the crowd started to boo Ti loudly. The noise bounced off the club's walls and drifted down the hallway, until it reached the ears of Howard Hughes who was just arriving with a gorgeous starlet at his side. Curious, Hughes excused himself from his date, stepped inside the banquet hall unnoticed, and stood in the shadows.

At the head table, Van Hauffwigin was visibly

upset. Trying to cover up any possible link between himself and Ti, he quickly screamed like a stuck pig, "Who is that man? What does he think he's doing?"

Seeing his old adversary and realizing Ti was on his turf, Jack said calmly to Van Hauffwigin, "Don't worry, I'll take care of him."

With a calming hand to the crowd, Jack motioned at Ti, and said, "Did you have a question for me, sir?"

"Yeah. I was just wondering how you can be called the finest golfer in the country–when the finest golfer in the country should be able to beat me! And I don't think you can, St. James."

The crowd roared its disapproval, and with his hands, Jack quieted them yet again.

Ti continued, "From what I found out earlier tonight, I would never have reached the first tee tomorrow. Some committee would have taken care of that."

A voice from the crowd yelled, "We don't want or need your kind around here!"

Alice stood against a wall watching in fascination. She did not notice Hughes was standing just next to her.

Ti continued, "But that's okay–tell you the truth, I don't cotton much to your country club medal play for shiny trophies, anyway. Kinda boring. What I really like is good old-fashioned, put-your-own-money-down match play."

Another voice from the crowd said, "Why don't you just get the hell out of here? This is a respectable place. We have rules against your type. You're nothing more than a cheap hustler!"

Ti smarted when he heard that, and the laughter from the crowd, but he continued. "Yeah. I'm a hustler. But there's nothing cheap about me. And another thing. I have lived by a hard and fast rule that I will never–let me repeat–absolutely never break. And that is–I will not hustle some poor guy who might blow his brains out because he lost the money he was going to use to buy shoes for his kids. No sir! I would never do that. Now, how many of you so-called reputable businessmen, who smile and sing your amens at church on Sunday, can say that?"

He looked around the room where all of these wealthy, self-indulgent people were gathered so comfortably. As he did, he thought back to that Arkansas river, and Buck Bostwick–and he realized that things never really changed. There are the "haves" and the "have nots." And when it was all said and done, it was still just a matter of trying to do what his Mother had taught him–it was still just a question of surviving.

Alice smiled softly and looked proudly at Ti as he faced the mob alone, and continued, "Now back to the question at hand. The truth is–I think I am the best damn golfer in this room. And maybe in the whole damn country!"

There was general laughter from this comment.

"And I'll tell you what," he said. "I'm willing to put my money, right where my mouth is. Now, you may not approve of me–much less respect me–but what I've got in here," he said, as he patted the brown suitcase, "I know each and every one of you respects."

He slammed his suitcase down on a table, popped it open, then held the contents up, over his head, for all to see. And see they did. And when they saw stack after stack of hundred dollar bills–a murmer filled the room.

The point being made, Ti said, "You are all good businessmen, so you should appreciate what a great opportunity I'm about to offer you."

"Let's hear it," one intrigued voice said.

"I'll play Jack St. James tomorrow–match play–for any amount you name. You can back your boy to the limit, and I'll cover it. All I ask is to be able to lay side bets as often–and for as much–as I want, and that no bet I make can be refused." Then he pointed at Jack, and concluded. "Me against the finest golfer in the country. It's that simple. So, are there any takers?"

The eyes of all the men at the head table lit up like slot machines as they quickly huddled with Jack.

"Hell! That's a guaranteed sure thing, Jack," said Van Hauffwigin. "I'll cover all that bet by myself!"

But all of the other men at the head table frantically gathered around Jack, as if he were a prized bull and this was a bidding war.

"Me too!" said Don Carter. "I'm in!"

"Don't forget me!" begged Craven-Finch. Jack nodded at his associates, then turned back to the microphone and with an egomaniacal smile said, "Thomas. You've got a bet!"

The elegant diners rose as one, and filled the banquet hall with a deafening chant, "Jack! Jack! Jack! Jack! Jack! Jack! Jack! Jack! Jack!"

Jack stood, overwhelmed–loving it–and with arms raised, accepted the accolades. There was just a hint of a smile on Ti's face.

Alice could only stare at the mob with amazement, and a little fear.

Chapter 21

Birds of a Feather Don't Always Flock Together.

The next morning, excited El Rancho members, along with Jack's biggest backers–Van Hauffwigin, Carter, Craven-Finch and Cumminski–crowded around the confident Jack St. James, as he signed autographs and made small talk with several women hell-bent on flirting with him.

Next to Ti stood Alice, who carried the brown suitcase full of money, and a young man, Jimmy, his assigned caddy.

"Good luck, Mr. Thomas," said Jimmy.

"Call me Ti. And, believe me, Jimmy, luck will have nothing to do with this."

Alice smiled and kissed Ti on the cheek, while nearby, Carter, Cumminski, Craven-Finch, and Van Hauffwigin smiled and gazed at Jack with special admiration.

Van Hauffwigin announced to Carter and Cumminski, "Jack has that unmistakable look of a winner. Someday I'll let you both read the thesis I wrote while a student at Cal. State Tremor. It was titled–Winners and Losers. In it, I theorized that winners are smart enough to never let their egos lead them outside of their zone of superiority– as the philosopher, Baboonski, put it."

"Obviously Titanic has drifted into his zone of stupidity," said Cumminski. They all laughed, but stopped quickly as Van Hauffwigin walked onto the 1st tee and began the proceedings.

"Ladies and gentlemen. As you know, our medal tournament has been postponed. Instead, today we will see match play. Five thousand dollars a hole, ten thousand dollars for birdies, and fifteen thousand dollars for eagles. Side bets–of any amount–must be accepted and covered, or the match is forfeited. And, this match is between Jack St. James..." he was interrupted by loud applause and whistling. Finally, order was restored and he continued, "... Between Jack and Alvin Thomas– also known in some circles as Titanic."

Only a murmur drifted through the crowd, no applause.

"If there are no questions," Van Hauffwigin concluded, "Mr. St. James won the flip–so gentlemen, play away."

With a wave of his hand and a slight bow, Jack acknowledged the applause, teed up his ball, and then swung, sending his ball roaring off into the distance. The gallery roared its approval.

Ti teed up his ball, swung and his ball exploded off his driver. Of course, Jimmy, Ti's caddy, had never seen Ti play and knew little about him really. It was just a job, and as he strained to see the ball flying away–far off into the distance– he innocently smiled and commented, "Gosh, Ti. That's at least twenty yards further than Mr. St. James's ball."

"Come on, Alice," Ti smiled and said. "This is the day I've been waiting for. It's gonna be fun, because I don't have to hold anything back!" She walked down the fairway contentedly with Ti as Jimmy followed just behind.

The first hole was routine. Ti and Jack both hit their iron shots near the pin, sank their putts, and hole #1 was history.

Hole #2 was just an uneventful. Whock. Whock. Two great tee shots. Splat. Splat. Two great iron shots. Two simple putts were ahead, but just after Ti made his, a little thing happened.

Jack had a short, two-foot putt, and casually looked at Ti–motioned to his short putt–and said, "This one good with you?" Then he started to reach down and pick his ball up, but stopped, when he heard Ti casually say, "It's good when it's in the hole." So, Jack smiled. *There's not one ounce of class in him,* he thought. Then he shrugged and tapped the simple putt in.

But, the point had been made–and not too subtlety–that unlike most days in Jack's life, today there would be no gimmies, no freebies and no quarter.

Hole #3 started off exactly as the two previous holes. Whock. Whock. Routine drives for both men. But, as they walked down the fairway, Ti turned to Jack, and said, ever so casually, "Hey! St. James." Jack looked over at him, as Ti said intensely, "Let's play some golf."

With that, the match really started in earnest. It was poetry in motion. And, years later when an old Jimmy would tell the story, he would recall how everything turned to slow motion in his mind. Not one thing stood out–but it was like a parade of images–like Jack's unexpected, serendipitous putt, dropping in on the 4th hole.

That uncharacteristic grin from Ti, as he covered Jack's putt with his own difficult one from fifteen feet.

Jimmy would recall how the feelings of the two competitors were bared that day–the looks magnified. How the events of the day seemed to blend those esoteric emotions and special feelings– the ups and downs–the good, the bad–the one that should have dropped–but didn't. The one one that should not have dropped–but did, somehow.

Those old rich guys there that day–with names like Cumminski, Craven-Finch, and Van Hauffwigin–he remembered their fists in the air, silently cheering St. James. How the biased country club crowd pounded Jack on the back as he walked between holes.

When asked years later to recount anything–anything at all–about Ti that day, Jimmy just recalled how rock solid and steady he was. A real, honest-to-God predator. And, those eyes. Eyes so intense that they seemed to bore right through you.

But the match–that's what they all asked him to be specific about. "Sure," he always told them. "It was full of great shots." And even though those pictures were all clearly stuffed away in his memory–still, for the life of him, he could never remember anything really extraordinary about the match, or more important, exactly when the match started to change. But boy–did it ever.

Jimmy did surprise most people by remembering Alice so well. After all, he had only met her that one day, and never saw her again. But still, he remembered that beautiful woman–steadfastly beside her man–and tough. She watched as Ti worked his magic on the course that day, as she handled the money, and covered all the wagering Ti made, from her traveling office–that nondescript, brown suitcase. Jimmy remembered she had even–as a lark–haggled some small bets from the crowd herself, and had later said, "It was fun."

Yes, Jimmy remembered all of that. And, it was fun.

But on that day of the match, Jack St. James watched as Ti made yet another putt. And then, a slow smile spread across Alice's face. Somehow, she knew something was happening. She just felt it.

Even though Craven-Finch and Van Hauffwigin shook hands as Jack hit a shot, stiff on the pin–right then, there was–even to them–a subtle feeling of change. A feeling, and nothing more, that a winner was emerging. And one was, because just then, at just that exact moment, Ti struck an iron–and struck it just so–that although it hit the green far beyond the hole, it danced–like a puppet–back, back until it started rolling slowly and steadily toward the pin, where it finally stopped within inches of the hole.

That was when that small, small look, first appeared on Jack's face. Just a look. A small thing. But a telling one. Because for all practical purposes, from that moment on, the match was really over. Jack was like a fighter who had thrown every punch he possessed at another fighter, and yet, that other fighter just refused to go down. And now, Jack had nothing left. Absolutely nothing else in his bag of tricks to pull out. And, worst of all, he knew it.

So, Jack did not answer that magnificent approach shot by Ti. He just could not. And when Ti sank his putt, he won the hole. And that meant that Carter, Cumminski, Craven-Finch, and Van Hauffwigin all had to dig into their wallets to cover a bet–for the first time that day–but not the last.

Ti started to attack like a shark. With Jack looking at a simple ten foot putt, Ti made a side bet of ten thousand dollars–and Jack missed badly.

With Jack in a sand trap, Ti bet him fifteen thousand dollars he could not get out of the trap in one stroke. Jack chili-dipped his shot, nearly breaking his sand iron in the process.

With Jack on the tee box of a simple par-three hole, Ti bet him a staggering twenty thousand dollars that he would not, in fact could not, even hit his ball, as he put it, "... Anywhere on that big damned green in front of all your friends over there." And as if Ti had willed it, Jack not only missed the green, but also the ball–entirely. A whiff!

Then those images flooded by again:

Ti's face as he smelled blood.

The look he gave St. James.

The way St. James avoided his gaze.

Carter, Cumminski, Craven-Finch, and Van Hauffwigin grimacing as they saw and felt it all–slipping quickly away.

The flood of missed opportunities. Missed shots.

Domination.

All the while the flags of each hole floated by: 7 – 8 – 9 – 10 – 11 – 12 –

A sign saying "We Love You Jack" in the grass being walked on by Jack's fair-weather fans, who came to see a walk-in-the-park, but were now, disgustedly, leaving him in droves.

Finally, the only ones who were left were the few with the big money on the line—Carter, Cumminski, Craven-Finch, and Van Hauffwigin—and a few others. But it was the "hard cores," with lots of money to lose, who were mad. Bitter.

They watched with little emotion left as St. James missed a green. Couldn't make his sandie out of a trap. Finally—total submission.

It was like mop-up time on a battlefield in a war. Ti was just making all the money he could before the bonanza was over. Making bet-after-bet with a deflated Jack, who had no choice but to accept—even though he had no chance, and in fact, no desire left.

Jack was not only losing big for his backers, but he was also coming apart at the seams. Finally, drenched in nervous sweat, and not able to take it either physically or mentally anymore, he glared at Ti with fear and hatred and shouted, "This isn't golf! You've turned it into a fucking circus!"

Ti just smiled knowingly, and said, "Jack. You should have thought of that before you took it upon yourself to go after me and my wife."

Jack ducked his head and walked quickly away—trying not to hear the truth. But like a panther, Ti quickly caught him and said, "Fifteen grand you don't get out of that sand trap."

Alice was concerned. Revenge may have been sweet, but she did not want to see Ti become bitter like the rest–especially when he should have been enjoying a great and profitable victory.

She joined Ti and whispered, "Ti. Let's take our winnings and go home. Enough is enough."

"With them it's never enough. Why should I be any different? Why should I let them off the hook now that I finally got it going my way?" he said, revealing his instincts, like those of a wild animal on a feeding frenzy–enjoying the smell of blood and flushed with the moment of kill.

He was back at St. James now. In his face with, "I said fifteen grand, Jack. Now hit that damn ball out of the trap and make yourself and your friends some money– pal–" he added sarcastically.

With absolutely no conviction, Jack took a half-hearted swing at his ball, buried in the sand trap, and babied the shot–badly miss-hitting it. As the ball fell back into the trap, Jack exploded, and broke his sand iron over his knee.

Jack's backers, numb from writing check-after-check, hardly noticed Jack's latest outburst. But one man did. A man who walked with a limp and a cane. It was Gerald St. James, who had just arrived. And when he saw what was happening to Jack–and the man who was doing it–he stepped from the crowd, his face contorted in hatred. With his cane he demanded Van Hauffwigin's attention as he said angrily, "How did you let this happen?"

"I can assure you that we have all lost today– big," said Van Hauffwigin, quietly and bitterly.

"Titanic won't stop–he's after blood."

"How much have you lost so far?" Gerald demanded.

"Our best estimate is something over one-hundred and ninety thousand," a dejected Van Hauffwigin muttered. "Hard to tell the way he keeps running up the side bets."

Gerald looked in the direction of his tortured son and said, "I'll have to take matters into my own hands."

"What can you do?" said a mystified Van Hauffwigin.

"Teach you simpering, self-indulgent morons something about business–and life. I'm going to make sure this match never happened."

"You mean there's a chance we can get out of this? Get our money back?" Van Hauffwigin said in utter amazement.

"I could care less about your losses," said Gerald with disdain. "I just want to get my son home and convince him this was a freak show– an aberration."

"How? How are you going to..."

"With an old Howard Hughes trick. I'm going to buy this tournament," Gerald said with a wicked smile. Then he walked out on the fairway, and like a policeman directing traffic, used his cane as he motioned for the attention of the two players.

"There's no need to continue–this match is

over!" said Gerald directly to Ti, with obvious satisfaction.

"It's over when the play is over and the money is all paid out," Ti said coldly. *What in the hell is the old bastard up to?* he wondered.

"Oh, no, it's over all right. And, your very own rule did you in, Thomas. How did you so cleverly put it? Any bet that's made–must be covered?"

"I don't know what you're getting at. We've covered every bet," Ti said as Alice nodded her agreement, and started to show the tote sheet.

But Gerald simply raised his hand to stop it all. "You've matched every bet–except the one I am now putting on the table. A side bet covering the remaining five holes. A bet for–one million dollars!" he said as he took a personal check from his coat pocket. "I can and will fill my check out right now. However–and correct me if I am wrong–but Thomas, I don't think you've got that kind of money in that little brown suitcase? Correct?"

Alice closed her eyes in utter despair. *We should have quit while we were so far ahead,* she thought. Ti could only stare at Gerald in disbelief.

"Well then. If you can't cover it, this match is forfeited. Canceled. It never happened," said Gerald, as Van Hauffwigin, Carter and all the rest of Jack's early backers were all smiles. It was truly a miracle. Thanks to Gerald St. James, they had been rescued from the jaws of a certain financial bloodbath.

But, from out of nowhere, stepped a tall, dark-haired man, a man named Howard Hughes. He calmly walked over to Gerald and said, "St. James. It happened all right. And I want everybody to remember it. It's been a long time since I've seen a bunch of rich, pampered, over-protected social butterflies get their wings clipped like this. So, I'll tell you what." He smiled at Ti and Alice. "I'll cover that million dollars! And a little more if you need it. But there is a limit to what even I can do."

Hughes waited, looked the expectant crowd over carefully, then finished. "I can't go a penny over fifty million."

The only thing worse than actually getting your financial brains beaten out, is believing that you have somehow been miraculously spared from that fate, but then, at the last second, finding out that you were wrong–and yes, your financial brains will be beaten out after all. And that is exactly the emotional roller-coaster which was ridden by Carter, Cumminski, Craven-Finch, and Van Hauffwigin in the span of just a few, heart-stopping moments that day. And, when they found out that their worst fears had finally been confirmed, each melted like an ice cube on a hot summer day.

Van Hauffwigin barely had breath left in him, but he found it to beg, "Howard. Please. Please! Reconsider. Why back him against us? After all, you pay your dues here. You're a member. You're one of us!"

Hughes looked at Van Hauffwigin and the rest of his cronies with utter disgust. "You band together–gang up against him and try to drive him out–and when you think you've finally found a way to beat him, you try to drive him under–and when you can't, you scream like a bunch of stuck pigs. Why? Because you hate anyone who goes his own way. And he can–because he's better than all of you–in every way. Now I may be a little unorthodox, even a little eccentric–and yes, I may have inherited what I started with–just like you. But there's a difference. A big one. I don't sit on what I have, just waiting for someone else in my family to die so I can get more, that I didn't earn. I decided a long time ago to use what I have to create things. To build things. So, I don't need to pull anyone else down just to make myself look better. I'm not a chicken shit. No, I'm not one of you."

The truth hurt Gerald more than anyone that day. He closed his eyes for a moment in resignation, then like a general leaving the scene of a just concluded battle, he slowly said, "Gentlemen, it appears I have been trumped, and so I will retire from the field. I suggest you pay your debts and do the same."

Then to Jack, he said, "Let's go, son."

Red-eyed and thoroughly destroyed, Jack said quietly, "Sorry, father."

"Forget it, Jack. You never had a chance–I never gave you one." Then he, Jack and the rest started back to the club to lick their wounds.

Ti walked over to Hughes, extended his hand and said with great relief, "Thanks."

However, to a man who owned an oil well servicing business, a movie studio, dated beautiful Hollywood starlets, and did about anything else he wanted, this had not been that big a deal. In fact, just another one. So, his mind had already raced on to other things, and one of them involved a question that Hughes had been pondering–a question that only Ti could answer.

"You know, I have a serious interest in the aviation business," Hughes said. "So, I have studied aerodynamics, thrust, lift–things like that. And, I think I pretty well understand how airplanes are able to fly. But–I have absolutely no idea how you are going to hit that five hundred yard drive I've been hearing about. Want to tell me how you're going to hit a golf ball that far?"

Ti smiled and said mysteriously, "Well, no. But, if you come to New York, I'll show you."

Chapter 22

Drive For Show.
Drive For Dough.

The next week, on the morning which Ti had picked, it was clear, and very, very cold on Long Island. And it felt even colder on the fourteenth tee box at the Long Island Country Club, where Howard Hughes and Ti stomped their feet to stay warm, as Daryl looked on from his car. Alice, George, the Professor, Flynn and the reporter, Turner, all huddled together, shivering in the cold, as they pulled their coats around themselves and tried to stay warm.

"Damn! This is a hell of a lot colder than winter in Southern California," Hughes said. "Normally I wouldn't be caught dead on a golf course when it's ten degrees, but I'm glad I came. Now I see why St. James decided to pay up and leave early, instead of hanging around and being embarrassed again." He laughed, then said to Ti, "Well–you might as well go ahead and get this thing over with."

After a little difficulty, Ti finally teed his ball

up in the frozen ground, and leisurely took two practice swings to stretch out his cold, tight muscles. Then he addressed the ball, and said formally, "I said I would hit a five hundred yard drive from the tee box on the fourteenth hole here at the Long Island Country Club, and I am here today, to do that very thing."

Ti then turned one hundred and eighty degrees–away from the direction of the green–until he was facing the lake, directly behind the tee box. Then, with a smile, he took the club back and drove the ball far out on the shallow lake which was now– as it had been for awhile–frozen solid.

Hughes watched with Ti as the ball hit the ice way out there, and ran like a rabbit, away–away into the distance. Hughes said, "Yep. It'll go five-hundred yards all right. Hell, looks to me like it might go a damn mile."

And Hughes may very well have been right, for way out on that frozen lake, the ball was almost getting its second wind, as it soared out over the ice, hit with a thonnnng–and then bounded, high in the air, headed for parts unknown.

Somewhere way out there–beyond the sight of Ti and Hughes–a solitary fisherman held his rod and reel over a hole cut in the ice. Suddenly, he was startled, as a golf ball–of all things–came rushing toward him and then quickly on by, heading for the far shore.

Back on the fourteenth tee box, Ti, Hughes,

Alice, George, Flynn, the Professor and Turner, all laughed. Suddenly, from out of nowhere, a photographer rushed up, aimed quickly and snapped a picture of Hughes, just as Ti turned away, shielding his face.

"Thanks pal," the photographer said, as he smiled happily and ran away.

Hughes shrugged and said, "What are you gonna do? It's a pain in the ass but my studio P.R. guys say it's good for business. Happen to you a lot, Ti?"

"Never! Publicity is like the kiss of death in my business," said a disgusted Ti.

There was little left to say or do, so they all headed for the warmth of their cars, except for Ti who walked with Hughes toward Daryl, who had Hughes's car door open and waiting.

Hughes was laughing as he said, "Out in California–and that is where you will meet them all–this fellow at my movie studio wanted to bet me he could hit a golf ball a long ways. You know what he had in mind?"

He didn't wait for Ti to answer. "He was going to tee that ball up, and hit it down a road! A damned road like Sunset Boulevard or something! Like I couldn't figure that one out? Now what kind of idiot would take a bet like that? Hitting a golf ball down some kind of man-made surface–just to win a few bucks–is just chicken shit!"

Both men laughed. It was time for Ti to ask

Hughes something that had been bothering him. "Howard. Why do you hang around those goofy, toothy-grinning, 'please don't hurt my feelings or ask me to risk any of my own money,' society boys?"

Hughes looked at Ti with resignation and quietly said, "Maybe I don't have much of a choice." Then he brightened and said, "Say, if you ever want to play some golf, come on out to California again. We'll tee 'em up!" But then with mock seriousness, he added, "But Titanic–I won't play golf against you. I'll play with you."

Hughes roared with laughter, got into his car, and Daryl closed the door. But Hughes quickly rolled down the window, leaned out and said, "So long Titanic. Uh–it's Thomas, isn't it?" He extended his hand to Ti.

"Right," Ti said proudly, as he shook his hand. "Alvin Clarence Thomas, from Rogers, Arkansas."

Hughes smiled, gave Ti a small salute, motioned to Daryl, and they drove away.

———————————

As Ti and Alice drove back to New York, Alice had a frown on her face as she studied Ti for a long while. Finally, she said sternly, "And why didn't you tell me how you were going to do it?"

"A secret's only a secret as long as one person knows it," Ti said, never taking his eyes off the road.

"Why, I could have pretended I didn't know! I'm an actress! A good one!"

"Not that good," Ti said good naturedly.

At the same time, inside the Hughes car, Daryl looked back in his rear view mirror at his boss. Smiling, he shook his head and said, "Interesting fellow, that Titanic."

Hughes just nodded, deep in thought.

Daryl continued, "But, such a fuss about driving a golf ball five-hundred yards. It all just seems so silly to me."

"Maybe so, Daryl," said Hughes. "But that's the stuff of which legends are made."

Chapter 23

So Long.
It's Been Good
to Know You.

The next day, Grand Central Station was especially busy as holiday travelers flocked to the train station to reach loved ones far away.

Ti and Alice stood outside their compartment, shivering while trying to say goodbye to their friends. George, Flynn, the Professor, and Turner– all looking a bit sad–waited in line to see them off.

"It seems like we're always saying goodbye to the ones we love the most," Alice said through tears.

A whistle blew, signaling the near departure of their train.

"Sure I can't talk you into staying?" George said, almost choking up himself. "It's just not gonna be the same around here without the two of you."

Ti said, "George, it's just time for Alice and me to head on to where the climate's a little warmer–and folks don't know me so well."

"Back to California?" Flynn guessed.

"Naw. I don't think we've got the right image for that place," Ti said disgustedly. "I was thinking that after we stop by my Mother's place in Arkansas, we might just head on down to Texas. Plenty of golf courses and money down there–and the kinda boys that'll bet on anything–as long as it's a sure thing," he said, smiling.

George appealed to Alice. "Can't you talk him out of it?"

"Out of it? I finally found a part I could play the rest of my life–even if it is a road show!" she said, using her best Barrymore impersonation.

She kissed George affectionately on the cheek saying, "Be careful." Then she walked over to the Professor as Ti talked to George.

"Well, you finally got your wish," George said to Ti. "You finally got to meet Howard Hughes. Sorry he's not going to make you one of the big rich."

Ti gave George a warm look and said, "You know, I finally found out something. I really don't give a damn about being like one of those millionaires."

"No kidding?" George said, stunned.

"No, I just want to live like one."

George smiled and understood.

The Professor took Alice's hand and looked at her fondly, as he would a daughter. They were both startled by Ti's uncharacteristic laughter during his conversation with George.

The Professor nodded at Ti and said, "Well, just look at him. So happy you'd think he was going through his second childhood!"

"Professor. Maybe it's his first," Alice said pointedly. The Professor nodded his deep understanding. Then he added, "He's far luckier than most men who are forced to lead lives of quiet desperation. Yes, you and Mr. Ti are both lucky. You will have rich–interesting lives. Now, go enjoy them!"

Alice teared up again, looked thankfully at the Professor and gave him a kiss.

The conductor's voice sounded a familiar cry of, " 'Board! All aboard!" Sounds of steam hissing, bumps of railroad cars, and wheels grinding signaled that the train was about to leave.

Alice quickly kissed both Turner and an embarrassed Flynn, who said, "Now you take care of that boy, Alice. He's a good one. My best!"

Ti had worked his way down the line with considerably less emotion, and he and Alice were preparing to step aboard the train, when the Professor came rushing over, waving a newspaper in his hand. "Mister Ti. I forgot! Look!" he said excitedly, as he pointed at the newspaper. "The photographer who snapped your photo with Hughes–they spelled your name wrong in *The Times*."

He read aloud to Ti and Alice, "Pictured above, Howard Hughes, with an even more illusive person, Titanic Thompson. Thompson is the one with his face covered."

The Professor handed Ti the paper. He and Alice looked closely at the photo of Hughes and him, and sure enough, Ti did have his face covered. And, the name was wrong.

"They didn't get your picture, and, they put the wrong name down!" said the Professor.

"Thompson, huh?" said Ti. "All of New York will think my name is Thompson? Titanic Thompson?"

"I thought you'd get a kick out of that," said the Professor. "You've created a whole new character, and–a little misdirection, maybe?"

Ti thought for a second, then said to Alice, "Titanic Thompson one day. Alvin Thomas the next. Think that might confuse them for a while?"

"I wouldn't be at all surprised," said an amused Alice.

"Then, Titanic Thompson it is!" Ti said as Alice nodded her agreement. But she quickly added, "As long as I am still legally Mrs. Alvin Thomas."

Ti smiled and kissed her. "No problem,

Alice," he said. "I'll just be acting, playing a part like you."

They both stepped up into the stairwell of the train, then turned back and waved goodbye to their friends.

As the train slowly pulled away, it carried for the first time, a brand new character named Titanic Thompson, and his beautiful, happy wife, Alice.

Back at the train station, the friends all looked after the departing train in the distance. Then looked at the newspaper the Professor displayed. They all smiled and agreed, Titanic Thompson was a terrific name for a new character.

As they all turned to leave, George stopped Turner, and said, "You're the reporter. I have a question for you. Actually two."

"Shoot," said Turner.

"Well, first—and hypothetically speaking—if you could write only one story about Alvin Thomas—Titanic Thompson—which one would it be? One of the golf matches he won here in New York against the blue bloods—or better still—how he won it?" he said tapping his head.

Turner shook his head, "no."

"Maybe the way he stood up in front of that bunch in Los Angeles at El Rancho?" George asked.

Again, Turner shook his head "no."

"Or maybe the way he carved up Jack St. James like a Christmas turkey?"

Turner shook his head "no," yet again.

"No?" George said. "Then it would have to be...?"

"The five hundred yard drive," Turner said with conviction. "That's what I'd write about. What else! It was amazing the way he planned it– and did it."

George had been playing a game. And Turner knew it.

"And, the second question?" Turner asked.

"The really important one," George said. "In the story you'd write, describing the five hundred yard drive, what would be your headline?"

"Oh, I get it," said Turner. "You want me to tell you the headline I'd write, for an article of mine, which will probably never be published?"

"Exactly," said a devilish George.

"Simple!" Turner said. "There's only one headline to describe it, because it was truly a– stroke of genius!"

George just smiled, slapped Turner on the back and said, "Perfect, my friend. Perfect!"

As the two men walked out of Grand Central Station and back into their lives, Ti and Alice stood on the rear platform of their train, again traveling to meet their destiny–no matter where or what it proved to be. As they looked back at the city of New York–their old friend and foe–everything seemed very right to both of them.

"Burrr! Should have worn my gloves," Alice

said as she smiled and snuggled closer to Ti. She casually slid a bare hand into one of his overcoat pockets. "I love cold weather."

"And hot weather–and rainy weather–and windy weather," he said. "Truth is–I haven't run into any kind of weather you don't like. You got to watch out for changing weather, Alice. Weather can turn on you–fast!"

Add weather to his list of obsessions, she thought as she noticed he was warming a little too eagerly to the subject.

"Just wait 'til we hit tornado-alley down around Oklahoma and Texas this spring. Why I've seen clouds boil up so fast there wasn't a place safe for man or beast–pitch-black days as dark as night–destruction like you can't hardly imagine. And you know why, Alice?"

No, she thought. *But I've got a feeling I'm about to find out.*

"You just can't hide from a funnel a mile wide. See one–and you can count on homes being blown away and more misery than..."

She was now desperate to change the subject.

Mercifully–she felt something in his coat pocket. "Oh good," she said as she brought out a bag of peanuts, fished one out and jiggled it in her hand for a second. She looked puzzled. "My God! Ti, feel this thing!" She handed him the peanut. "I'm not kidding. That may be the heaviest peanut in the world!"

With a raised eyebrow, he put the peanut–as well as the bag–back into his coat pocket.

"Well, Alice. Now there are peanuts...and then there are... *peanuts*."

She pointed at the one in his coat pocket. "Uh, and that one is...?"

"Well, think of it as more like an insurance policy...if we should ever need it."

"Huh?" she said, totally confused.

"Alice, sometimes out on the road, you run into unexpected financial emergencies." He could see she did not have a clue. *No,* he thought. *She still isn't ready for the peanut story.* "Forget it. I'll explain it all later."

But, after being shut out of the five hundred yard drive setup, Alice wasn't about to forget it. "Look, at least you could tell me what..."

But she saw that Ti wasn't listening. He was distracted. With a sigh of resignation, she looked up as he pointed out something to her–high in the sky.

It was a flock of migrating geese, and they etched a nearly perfect V, in silhouette against a huge ball of white flame which was burning on the horizon.

Titanic Thompson
Stroke of Genius

A Great Read.

*"I found your book engrossing, fascinating,
eminently readable, very well written." - M. Bell*

*"I really enjoyed this book.
This would make a great Movie." - M. Widener*

" A fun read." - M. Weaver

*" Well written and very entertaining. I was sorry
that it had to end, and I am looking forward
to the next one." - D. Horne*

"A real page turner." - G. Hinson

A Great Gift.

To inquire about discounts for volume orders,
email: info@titanicthompson.com